Is It OCPD or OCD?

Telling apart the disorder of doubt and the disorder of control, and why the difference changes the treatment

Evie Dove Huynh

Decoding the Overlap, Book 1

The Decoding the Overlap Series, for the questions that come before the diagnosis.

This book is provided for general educational and informational purposes. It is not a diagnostic instrument, a treatment plan, or a substitute for medical or mental-health advice, diagnosis, or treatment from a qualified professional. Reading or completing the exercises does not establish whether any person has OCD, OCPD, both conditions, or another condition.

No particular result is promised. Mental-health assessment and treatment depend on individual history, symptoms, context, risk, medical factors, and professional judgment. Readers are responsible for deciding how to use the information and for seeking qualified care when needed. If there is an immediate risk of harm or a mental-health emergency, contact local emergency services or an appropriate crisis service.

Names, cases, and scenarios used to illustrate patterns are composites created for educational purposes. They are not intended to portray, diagnose, or misrepresent any identifiable person or organization.

ISBN: 978-1-911838-64-7

Table of Contents

Preface

Research and clinical guidance treat obsessive-compulsive disorder and obsessive-compulsive personality disorder as distinct conditions, yet their names invite confusion. Both can involve repetition, exactness, checking, rules, difficulty stopping, and costly attempts to get things right. A description of behavior on its own can therefore be a poor guide to what is happening underneath it. The more useful questions concern what starts the pattern, how the person relates to it, what the behavior is trying to accomplish, how broadly the pattern appears across life, and what a treatment is designed to change.

OCD is characterized by obsessions, compulsions, or both. Obsessions are intrusive thoughts, urges, or images that can generate distress, while compulsions are repeated behaviors or mental acts performed in response to an obsession or according to rules that feel difficult to resist. OCPD is a personality pattern marked by preoccupation with order, perfectionism, and control, with features that extend across settings and relationships. The familiar contrast between ego-dystonic and ego-syntonic can help describe a person's stance, but it is not a diagnostic test. OCD insight varies, and people with OCPD can recognize that their standards or control are costing them something.

The gap between those definitions and ordinary life is where confusion grows. A person may check a door because an intrusive possibility will not release its grip, or because checking is part of a defended standard about how responsible people should behave. A partner may see the same repeated act either way. A clinician may need much more than a symptom word such as perfectionism, control, reassurance, or checking to understand the process. When a previous diagnosis or treatment plan does not seem to explain the full pattern, the next useful step is not self-diagnosis. It is better observation.

This book provides a structured way to make those observations. The Five-Lens Difference Map asks you to examine Trigger, Stance, Function, Reach, and Treatment Fit. The chapters then apply those lenses to perfectionism, relationships, work, co-occurring patterns, exposure and response prevention, treatment mismatch, and preparation for a diagnostic review. Worksheets, paired cases, scripts, and a clinician visit pack turn the distinctions into material you can bring to an appointment.

Is It OCPD or OCD? is the first book in the Decoding the Overlap series, which begins with questions that often come before a settled diagnosis. The purpose of the series is not to replace assessment. It is to help readers describe confusing overlap with more precision. This volume is written primarily for adults who are unsure whether OCD, OCPD, both, or another explanation fits what they have been experiencing. Partners may also use it to describe patterns and impacts, without assigning a diagnosis to someone else.

No worksheet, case comparison, or self-observation in these pages can establish a mental-health diagnosis or determine the right treatment for a particular person. The material is educational and is not a substitute for individualized assessment or care from a qualified professional. If your symptoms are severe, rapidly worsening, or creating an immediate safety concern, seek appropriate professional or emergency support. The aim here is narrower and more practical: to help you arrive at the clinical conversation with better observations, better questions, and a clearer account of what does not fit.

Introduction: The Question Before the Label

Two mental health conditions can share four letters and still ask a clinician to solve different problems.

Obsessive-compulsive disorder, usually shortened to OCD, is organized around obsessions, compulsions, or both. Obsessions are intrusive and unwanted thoughts, urges, or images. Compulsions are repetitive behaviors or mental acts performed in response to an obsession or according to rules that feel difficult not to follow. The pattern becomes clinically important when it is time-consuming, distressing, or disruptive. Exposure and response prevention, usually shortened to ERP, is a well-supported psychological treatment for OCD. It works by helping a person face triggers while reducing the rituals and avoidance that keep the obsessive-compulsive cycle going (National Institute of Mental Health, 2023).

Obsessive-compulsive personality disorder, or OCPD, is different. It is a personality disorder characterized by a persistent pattern of preoccupation with order, perfectionism, and control, together with rigidity that causes problems in functioning or relationships. The pattern is broad rather than limited to a single symptom loop, and it typically reaches into decisions, work habits, delegation, standards, and relationships (Pinto et al., 2022).

Those definitions are clean on paper. Real lives are not.

A person with OCD may spend two hours checking a report because the thought of having made a catastrophic error will not release its grip. A person with OCPD may spend two hours checking the same report because submitting work that falls short of a personal standard feels irresponsible and unacceptable. A person with both conditions may do some of each. Someone with neither diagnosis may also be meticulous, anxious, perfectionistic, or controlling during a difficult period.

That is why this book does not ask you to count visible behaviors and add up a diagnosis. It asks a different set of questions.

The method used throughout is the **Five-Lens Difference Map**:

Lens	Question
Trigger	What starts the pattern?
Stance	How do you relate to the thought, rule, urge, or standard?
Function	What is the behavior trying to accomplish right now?
Reach	Is this a symptom loop, or a broad pattern across settings and years?
Treatment Fit	What mechanism is the intervention trying to change?

The map is an observation tool, not a diagnostic test. It cannot tell you that you have OCD, OCPD, both, or neither. It can help you replace a vague statement such as "I am obsessive" with information a clinician can actually examine.

Consider Maya, a composite example. She has spent years saying that she is "OCD about work." She rereads important emails, makes elaborate checklists, and struggles to let coworkers finish tasks in their own way. When she reads a description of OCD, the language about intrusive thoughts and rituals feels only partly familiar. When she reads a description of OCPD, the emphasis on perfectionism and control feels closer, but that also does not explain the nights when a sudden fear of harming someone sends her back to check the stove six times.

The useful question is not, "Which label sounds more like Maya?" The useful questions are narrower. What starts each behavior? Does she experience the thought or standard as something she wants to obey, something she fears, or both? What immediate job does checking perform? Does the pattern appear only around a handful of feared outcomes, or does it organize much of her working and relational life? What happens when a treatment targets one mechanism rather than the other?

Those are questions that can survive contact with a real assessment.

Why the Names Create So Much Confusion

The overlap in names is historically unfortunate for ordinary readers. "Obsessive-compulsive" appears in both, but the current diagnostic categories are not simply mild and severe versions of one condition. OCD is classified among obsessive-compulsive and related disorders. OCPD is a personality disorder. Clinical references explicitly distinguish them, even though they can co-occur (Pinto et al., 2022; Wheaton et al., 2022).

The confusion is strengthened by everyday language. People use "OCD" to mean neat, exacting, fussy, organized, repetitive, or particular. Those traits do not define OCD. Some people with OCD care very little about order. Their obsessions may concern harm, contamination, morality, relationships, religion, health, sexual themes, or mistakes. Their compulsions may be visible, such as checking, or mostly mental, such as reviewing, counting, neutralizing, or seeking certainty.

OCPD also gets flattened into "perfectionism." Perfectionism can occur in many conditions and in people with no mental disorder. OCPD concerns a pervasive pattern of perfectionism, order, and control that creates significant costs. A careful clinician looks at the pattern, duration, context, flexibility, and impairment rather than one attractive adjective.

The point of differential diagnosis is not to discover the perfect label for every human quirk. It is to distinguish clinically meaningful patterns well enough to guide care.

What This Book Can and Cannot Do

This book can help you notice distinctions that are easy to miss when you look only at behavior. It can help you keep a record without turning that record into a reassurance ritual. It can help you explain why a previous formulation seems incomplete. It can give a partner language for describing impact without diagnosing someone else. It can help you prepare questions about treatment fit.

It cannot diagnose you. It cannot determine whether a past clinician was wrong. It cannot tell you to begin, stop, or change psychotherapy or medication. If you are in treatment, use the material here as a way to improve the conversation with the professional who knows your history. If a question about safety, severe deterioration, or self-harm enters the picture, the task changes from differential reflection to getting timely professional or emergency support.

There is another limit worth making explicit. The evidence bases for the two conditions are not symmetrical. OCD has a large treatment literature, and ERP has strong support. OCPD has a much smaller treatment literature, with reviews repeatedly noting how limited the evidence remains (Pinto et al., 2022; Gecaite-Stonciene et al., 2022). That means a careful book should not manufacture a neat mirror image in which every OCD treatment has an equally established OCPD counterpart.

Clarity sometimes means admitting that one side of a comparison is less settled.

How to Use the Book

You can read straight through, but the book is designed to be worked with. Each chapter adds one kind of observation to your eventual one-page summary. Do not try to score yourself. The exercises deliberately avoid point systems because a high score on a homemade checklist is not a diagnosis.

When an exercise asks about a thought, rule, or behavior, choose one concrete example. "I need control" is too broad. "When a colleague edits my spreadsheet, I redo the formatting because I believe the structure is objectively better and errors are more likely if my system is not followed" gives you something to examine. "I check the door because an image of the house being burgled keeps returning and checking gives a few minutes of relief" gives you something else.

You may discover that different behaviors have different functions. That is useful information, not a failure of the map.

By the end, your goal is not to announce, "I figured out my diagnosis." Your goal is to be able to say something like this:

> *I have one set of behaviors driven by intrusive fears and temporary relief after checking. I also have a broader pattern of rigid standards and difficulty delegating that feels reasonable to me in the moment but creates conflict. I would like us to assess whether OCD explains all of this, whether OCPD traits or OCPD should be considered, and whether both could be present.*

That is a much better place to begin a clinical conversation.

Chapter 1: Two Names That Mislead

Daniel has a drawer for charging cables.

Not just a drawer with cables in it. Every cable is coiled the same way, grouped by connector, and labeled. His partner jokes that the drawer is "his OCD." Daniel laughs because that is what he calls it too.

Then, after a near miss on the highway, he begins seeing an image of his car drifting into a cyclist whenever he drives. The image is unwanted and horrifying. He starts circling blocks to make sure he did not hit anyone. At home, the cable drawer still looks exactly the same.

The two behaviors share a person and a reputation for exactness. They do not necessarily share a mechanism.

That is the first discipline of this book: **do not diagnose from the photograph**. A photograph captures what someone is doing. Differential diagnosis asks what process makes the behavior persist.

OCD Is Not a Personality Adjective

OCD is defined by obsessions, compulsions, or both. Obsessions are recurrent and persistent experiences that are intrusive and unwanted and that usually cause distress. Compulsions are repetitive behaviors or mental acts that a person feels driven to perform, often in an effort to reduce distress or prevent a feared event. The pattern must also meet clinical thresholds involving time, distress, or impairment, and a clinician considers other explanations (American Psychiatric Association, 2022).

Everyday speech often removes that mechanism. "I am so OCD" may mean "I like straight labels." A person can like straight labels without having OCD. A person can also have severe OCD and leave laundry in piles.

That matters because the stereotype distorts self-recognition. Someone whose OCD consists mainly of mental reviewing may conclude that OCD cannot be the answer because the kitchen is untidy. Someone who values order may conclude that OCD must be the answer because the kitchen is immaculate.

Neither conclusion follows.

The better question is whether there is an **OCD loop**: an intrusive obsession or sense of threat, followed by a compulsion, avoidance, reassurance seeking, or mental response that brings relief or a feeling of greater certainty, which then helps the cycle persist.

The loop can be quick. A thought appears. A person checks. Anxiety falls. Ten minutes later the doubt returns.

It can also be elaborate. A person worries that they may have offended a friend, rereads the conversation, reconstructs their tone, asks another friend what the message sounded like, searches online for signs of being a bad person, and then starts the review again because none of the answers feels final.

The content changes. The cycle is the useful part to notice.

OCPD Is Not "OCD but More Personality"

OCPD is organized differently. Clinical descriptions focus on a pervasive preoccupation with order, perfectionism, and control. Examples include becoming so focused on details or standards that tasks are hard to complete, giving work and productivity priority over leisure or relationships, having difficulty delegating unless others follow a preferred method, and showing rigidity or stubbornness (Pinto et al., 2022; Zimmerman, 2026).

A personality disorder is not simply a personality someone dislikes. The word *personality* in this context points to a durable pattern across thinking, feeling, relating, and behaving. Clinicians examine how broad and longstanding the pattern is and whether it causes meaningful impairment or distress.

That distinction protects against two mistakes.

The first is diagnosing ordinary conscientiousness. If Rafael likes deadlines, keeps careful records, and prefers to do his best work, that does not by itself indicate OCPD.

The second is dismissing costly rigidity as "just who I am." A trait can feel familiar and reasonable while still producing serious consequences. A manager can believe detailed oversight is necessary and still lose staff because no one is allowed to make a decision. A parent can believe there is one proper way to load a dishwasher and still create a home in which every small task becomes a test.

The pattern needs context.

The First Side-by-Side View

A comparison table is useful only if you treat it as a set of tendencies, not a test.

Question	OCD often involves	OCPD often involves
Core problem	Obsessions and compulsions	Pervasive perfectionism, order, and control
Typical immediate driver	Intrusive fear, doubt, disgust, incompleteness, or threat	Standards, rules, correctness, productivity, or control
Relationship to pattern	Frequently unwanted or distressing, though insight varies	Frequently experienced as reasonable or justified, though distress and self-criticism can occur
Scope	May cluster around particular obsessional themes	Usually broad across areas of life and longstanding
Behavior	Rituals, checking, avoidance, reassurance seeking, mental acts	Overcontrol, rigid standards, overwork, difficulty delegating, perfectionism
Treatment evidence	Strong evidence for CBT with ERP; medication may also be used	Smaller evidence base; psychotherapy approaches are used, but definitive treatment evidence is limited

The words *often*, *frequently*, and *may* matter. If you turn the table into a binary rule, it stops being clinically useful.

One example is insight. Many people with OCD recognize that their compulsions are excessive or do not make sense, but not everyone has the same level of insight. Likewise, a person with OCPD can be painfully aware of the costs of their rigidity. They may know that a marriage is deteriorating and still believe that their standard is correct.

The stance toward the pattern is evidence. It is not a verdict.

The Problem with Symptom Matching

Suppose Priya checks the front door five times.

If you know only that fact, you know almost nothing diagnostically.

Priya might be responding to an intrusive fear that she left the door unlocked and that someone will be harmed. She may know she watched herself lock it and still feel unable to trust the memory. Checking reduces anxiety briefly. That pattern could fit an OCD formulation.

Or Priya may believe every departure should follow a precise household security protocol. She may be irritated when family members do not complete it correctly. She does not check because a particular intrusive image is tormenting her. She checks because, from her point of view, responsible people follow the procedure. That broader stance may push an assessment toward OCPD features.

Or Priya may have lived through repeated burglaries and developed a safety habit in a high-crime environment. The behavior may be understandable in context and not indicate either diagnosis.

Or both OCD and OCPD may be relevant.

Visible behavior is the beginning of the question, not the end.

The Five-Lens Difference Map Begins Here

Take one behavior that has made you wonder about OCD or OCPD. Write it in a sentence that a camera could record.

Bad: "I am controlling."

Better: "I rewrite my coworker's reports after they submit them, even when the facts are correct."

Bad: "I obsess about mistakes."

Better: "After I send a tax form, I reread the saved copy for an hour because I keep thinking I entered the wrong number."

Now move through the five lenses.

Lens	Your notes
Trigger	What happened immediately before the urge or behavior?
Stance	Did the thought, rule, urge, or standard feel unwanted, doubtful, necessary, correct, or something else?
Function	What changed immediately after you acted? Less anxiety? More certainty? A restored sense of order? Prevention of someone else's "wrong" method?
Reach	Where else does this pattern appear, and how long has it been present?

Lens	Your notes
Treatment Fit	If you have received treatment, what process was it designed to change? What happened?

Do not force a clean answer. "I am not sure" is data. So is "sometimes it is fear and sometimes it is a standard."

Language Worth Dropping

Three casual phrases create more confusion than they solve.

The first is "I am OCD." OCD is a diagnosis, not a synonym for organized.

The second is "OCPD people like their symptoms." That is crude and often false in practice. A person may defend the rule and hate the consequences. They may feel proud of their work ethic and exhausted by it. They may believe their system is correct while wishing they could bend without feeling irresponsible.

The third is "If you know it is irrational, it is OCD." Insight can help a clinician understand a case, but insight varies in OCD and self-awareness varies in OCPD. A single question about whether something feels rational cannot carry the diagnosis.

Better language stays closer to observation:

"I get an intrusive thought that I caused harm, and I check until the anxiety drops."

"I believe there is a right way to do the task, and I have trouble letting another person use a different method."

"I can see that this rule is damaging the relationship, but I still feel the rule itself is justified."

"I know the fear is unlikely, but knowing that does not stop the urge to get certainty."

Those sentences tell you more than a label used as an adjective.

What to Carry Forward

The first chapter leaves you with a rule that will return throughout the book:

Same behavior does not mean same function.

Checking can be a compulsion. It can be a perfectionistic control strategy. It can be an ordinary safety behavior. It can serve more than one function in the same person.

For the next week, do not track every odd thought or habit. Choose three moments when an "OCD or OCPD?" question actually matters. Record what happened before, what you did, and what changed immediately afterward.

That small record will give Chapter 2 something real to work with.

A Better First Interview With Yourself

Before you search another symptom list, take one confusing behavior and answer six sentences.

"I do this when ..."

"Immediately before I do it, I notice ..."

"If I do not do it, I expect or fear ..."

"After I do it, I feel or believe ..."

"This pattern also appears in ..."

"The main cost is ..."

Notice how much harder these sentences are than "I am obsessive." That difficulty is useful. The language forces you to move from category words to sequence.

Suppose you write, "I recheck every invoice because I am perfectionistic." You still do not know much. Add the missing sequence: "After I send an invoice, I get a flash that I may have put the decimal in the wrong place. I reopen the file. Seeing the number lowers my anxiety for a few minutes. Then I wonder whether I looked at the right line." Now you have a possible obsession-compulsion process to discuss.

A different sequence might be, "I review every invoice because our team accepts work I consider sloppy. Once I have checked it against my system, I feel the work is finally at an acceptable standard. I also redo colleagues' schedules and reports because I do not trust their methods." Now the breadth and stance are different.

The exercise does not name either diagnosis. It makes the next question better.

The Name Is Not the Mechanism

A useful habit for the rest of this book is to replace diagnostic shorthand with mechanism language whenever you catch yourself using it.

Instead of "my OCD cleaning," say "the cleaning I do after contamination fears."

Instead of "my OCPD rules," say "the rules I defend even when other competent methods would work."

If a diagnosis is already established, you do not have to stop using it. The point is to keep the label from doing all the explanatory work.

Labels are most helpful after the process underneath them is visible.

Chapter 2: Follow the Pattern Underneath

A label usually arrives after a behavior has become noticeable.

"I check."

"I need things perfect."

"I cannot delegate."

"I get stuck on details."

Those statements are useful, but they are descriptions of the top layer. The Five-Lens Difference Map asks you to keep going until you can see the sequence underneath.

This chapter focuses on the first three lenses: Trigger, Stance, and Function. They are where two nearly identical behaviors often begin to separate.

Trigger: What Started This Particular Episode?

A trigger is not always a dramatic event. It may be an image, a bodily sensation, a line in an email, another person's mistake, an unfinished task, or the absence of a feeling you expected to have.

For OCD, a trigger can activate an obsession or an uncomfortable sense of uncertainty, threat, contamination, responsibility, wrongness, or incompleteness. The person may then perform a compulsion or avoidance behavior to reduce distress or prevent a feared outcome (National Institute of Mental Health, 2023).

For an OCPD pattern, the trigger may be a deviation from a rule, a loss of control, someone else's method, a perceived drop in quality, inefficiency, or a demand to be flexible. The reaction is often tied to standards and the conviction that a particular way is preferable or necessary (Pinto et al., 2022).

The trigger alone still does not decide the case.

Imagine that Marcus receives a spreadsheet with three inconsistent fonts.

In one version, the inconsistency sparks an intrusive fear: if this report looks careless, the client may cancel, staff may lose jobs, and it will be Marcus's fault. He reformats the sheet, checks it, then checks again because the feeling of certainty does not last.

In another version, Marcus thinks the file is objectively sloppy. He believes people should follow the template because professional work has standards. He spends an hour fixing it, then sends the colleague a detailed message about formatting rules. His distress is less about a feared catastrophe than about another person doing the work improperly.

The surface action is identical. The trigger begins to reveal the difference.

Stance: What Is Your Relationship to the Thought or Rule?

The terms **ego-dystonic** and **ego-syntonic** are common in explanations of OCD and OCPD.

Ego-dystonic means an experience feels inconsistent with the person's values, identity, or wishes. An intrusive thought such as "What if I secretly want to hurt my child?" may be horrifying precisely because it conflicts with what the person wants.

Ego-syntonic means a thought, rule, or behavior feels compatible with the person's values or self-concept. A standard such as "Important work should be done exactly this way" may feel not merely comfortable but morally or practically correct.

That distinction can be illuminating. It also becomes misleading when it is used as a one-question diagnostic test.

OCD insight varies. A person may be almost certain that a feared consequence is real, particularly when symptoms are severe. Clinical diagnostic systems recognize differing levels of insight in OCD (American Psychiatric Association, 2022). OCPD is not a state of cheerful agreement with every trait. People can become distressed by lost relationships, missed deadlines, exhaustion, conflict, or the realization that their standards have become costly.

So instead of asking only, "Does this feel like me?" use four narrower questions:

1. Do I want this thought, or did it arrive against my wishes?
2. Do I believe the rule is correct, even when I dislike its cost?
3. If the fear vanished, would I still want to perform the behavior this way?
4. If another competent person used a different method and nothing bad happened, would the difference itself still bother me?

Those questions do not diagnose. They make stance observable.

Function: What Does the Behavior Do in the Next Minute?

Function is the most practical lens in the book.

It asks what the behavior accomplishes immediately, not what you say it means in general.

A compulsion often reduces anxiety, doubt, disgust, guilt, or a sense of incompleteness. The relief may be brief. That short relief can make the ritual more likely to happen again the next time the obsession appears. This is one reason ERP focuses on changing the relationship between trigger and response rather than supplying more certainty (National Institute of Mental Health, 2023).

An OCPD behavior may restore order, preserve a standard, reassert control, prevent delegation, or remove the discomfort of another person's method. The relief is not necessarily "I am now safe." It can be "Now the job is being done correctly."

Compare two internal summaries:

"I checked because I could not tolerate the possibility that I had hit someone, and checking gave me a few minutes of relief."

"I checked because I do not trust other people to apply the standard correctly, and I wanted the final work to meet the standard."

They can coexist. But they point to different jobs.

Function Is Not the Same as Motive

Be careful with the word *motive*. It can sound accusatory, especially in relationships.

If a partner says, "Your motive is control," the conversation usually gets worse. Function is more neutral. It asks what the behavior changes in the system.

If Elena corrects how everyone loads the dishwasher, the immediate function may be restoring her preferred order. That does not tell you whether she is selfish, afraid, conscientious, overwhelmed, rigid, or simply convinced that her arrangement works better.

If Ben asks, "Are you sure you locked the door?" eight times, the function may be reassurance that lowers his fear temporarily. That does not mean he is deliberately demanding attention.

Describing function is not an accusation. It is a way to see reinforcement and pattern.

A Three-Column Record

For one week, try a brief record with only three columns.

Trigger	Response	Immediate result
Sent an email with a number in it	Reopened the sent message four times	Anxiety dropped, then doubt returned
Coworker used a different file structure	Reorganized the folder myself	Felt that the project was back under control
Partner questioned my rule about spending	Argued for forty minutes and produced a budget spreadsheet	Felt justified, partner withdrew
Intrusive image of contaminating a child	Washed hands again	Disgust and fear eased briefly

Notice what is not in the table: a diagnosis column.

The absence is intentional.

If you add "OCD" and "OCPD" too early, you will start sorting ambiguous experiences into the answer you expect. Collect the sequence first. Interpret it later with a clinician.

Watch for Mental Compulsions

OCD can be missed when compulsions are mostly internal.

A person may replay a memory to decide whether they acted immorally. They may silently repeat a phrase until it feels safe. They may compare feelings toward a partner, test whether a thought produces arousal, review evidence, pray in a ritualized way, or try to achieve certainty through analysis.

From the outside, the person may look thoughtful rather than compulsive.

This is one reason a simple comparison between "rituals" and "personality" is not enough. The ritual may be hidden, and the OCPD behavior may be visible. A good assessment asks what happens inside the sequence.

Reassurance seeking can also function as a compulsion. Family accommodation, including providing repeated reassurance or participating in rituals, can become part of the OCD cycle (American Psychiatric Association, n.d.).

If you notice that your record itself has become a certainty project, simplify it. Record one episode a day. Do not reread the entry to make sure it is "accurate enough." The tool should collect information, not become another ritual.

Look for Counterfactuals

A counterfactual asks what you would want if one part of the situation changed.

It is a useful observation technique because it separates the feared outcome from the standard.

For example:

"If I knew with complete certainty that no one would be harmed, would I still need to check this six times?"

"If I knew the client would be perfectly satisfied, would I still insist that the team use my exact formatting method?"

"If I knew the thought said nothing about my character, would I still mentally review it?"

"If the task could be completed to an acceptable level by someone else, would I still feel compelled to take it back because their method is wrong?"

Real life never gives complete certainty, so these are not experiments designed to prove a diagnosis. They are thought exercises that clarify what the behavior is protecting.

The Cost of Asking the Wrong Question

When readers try to distinguish OCD from OCPD, they often ask, "Which symptoms do I have?"

A better question is, "What process turns this trigger into this response?"

That shift matters because the same noun can hide different processes.

Perfectionism can become a compulsion when it is used to neutralize obsessional doubt. Perfectionism can be part of a pervasive OCPD pattern when standards, control, and rigidity organize many areas of life. Perfectionism can also appear in depression, eating disorders, anxiety disorders, autism, ADHD compensation, trauma-related coping, or ordinary personality. This book cannot settle those differentials, but it should keep them visible.

The goal is not to narrow your field of vision too early.

A Question to Take to Treatment

If you are currently in therapy and the work feels mismatched, do not begin by saying, "I think the diagnosis is wrong."

Try a mechanism question:

What do you think this behavior is doing for me, and which part of our treatment is meant to change that process?

A good answer should be more specific than "It treats anxiety" or "It treats perfectionism." It should connect the treatment to a formulation.

You can then add:

I notice that some of my checking is driven by intrusive fear and relief, but some of my rigidity feels more like a broad standard I believe is correct. Could we look at those separately?

That is the kind of information differential diagnosis needs.

Separate the First Minute From the Larger Story

People are good at explaining themselves after the fact.

That can make Function hard to see.

If you ask why you spent an hour revising a form, you may produce a broad answer: "I care about accuracy." The useful data may be in the first minute instead. Perhaps the first reopening followed a sudden image of a costly mistake. Perhaps the first correction followed irritation that someone ignored your template. Perhaps you were simply fixing an objective error.

For one episode, write only what happened in the first sixty seconds. Do not write the life story.

Then write what happened ten minutes later.

This split can reveal reinforcement. An action that buys immediate relief and then invites another round of doubt has a different shape from an action that restores a standard and ends when the work matches the rule.

Neither shape is exclusive to one diagnosis. The value is that you are no longer guessing from the noun.

Ask What the Behavior Requires From Other People

Function often becomes clearer when the behavior crosses a relationship.

Does the pattern require someone else to provide certainty?

Does it require them to follow your method?

Does it require them to avoid a trigger for you?

Does it require them to accept correction?

Does it require them to keep a real safety rule?

Write the demand as plainly as possible.

For example: "I need my partner to answer the same question until I feel certain" is different from "I need my partner to use my filing system because I believe other systems are wrong."

A clinician can learn from that difference. A partner can also describe it without making a diagnosis.

Chapter 3: The OCD Loop From Inside

OCD is often described with a list: contamination, checking, symmetry, unwanted thoughts.

Lists help people recognize possibilities, but they can also create a false picture. The condition is not defined by a particular theme. It is defined by the relationship among obsessions, distress, compulsive responses, avoidance, and impairment.

The easiest way to understand that relationship is as a loop.

Obsession Is More Than "Thinking a Lot"

In ordinary speech, people say they are obsessed with a television series, a new hobby, or a person they like. Clinical obsessions are different. They are recurrent thoughts, urges, or images experienced as intrusive and unwanted, commonly associated with anxiety or distress (American Psychiatric Association, 2022).

The content can be shocking because it collides with what the person cares about.

A gentle parent may get violent images. A careful driver may be tormented by doubt about a hit-and-run. A religious person may experience blasphemous thoughts. Someone deeply committed to a relationship may become trapped in questions about whether they love their partner "enough."

The presence of a thought does not reveal intent. Intrusive thoughts occur broadly in the population. In OCD, the problem is often the meaning assigned to the thought and the cycle of responses that follows.

Sofia has an image of pushing someone onto train tracks. The image disgusts her. She immediately asks herself why she had it. Then she scans for any sensation that could indicate desire. She remembers every angry moment she has had. She searches for stories about people who acted on violent thoughts. Each step is an attempt to solve the threat, but every step teaches her attention that the thought deserves more investigation.

The obsession gets a larger stage.

Compulsions Can Look Sensible

Some compulsions are easy to recognize: repeated washing, repeated checking, arranging, or counting.

Others look like responsible behavior.

A person rereads a contract ten times "to be safe." They ask a doctor the same question in several forms. They confess small mistakes to make sure they are not hiding anything. They ask a partner for reassurance about the relationship. They mentally reconstruct a conversation until it feels morally clean.

The difference is not whether the behavior could ever be sensible. It is how it functions in the cycle.

If the act repeatedly serves to neutralize distress, obtain certainty, prevent a feared catastrophe, or make an internal sense of wrongness go away, and if the relief keeps the pattern alive, a clinician may understand it as compulsive.

That is why reassurance can become part of OCD. The reassurance works for a moment. Then the doubt finds a new opening.

The Relief Trap

The OCD loop can be sketched in four steps:

Step	What happens
Trigger	A thought, image, sensation, situation, or uncertainty appears
Meaning	The experience is interpreted as threatening, significant, or requiring certainty
Response	The person checks, avoids, neutralizes, reviews, seeks reassurance, or performs another compulsion
Short-term effect	Distress or uncertainty falls, reinforcing the response

ERP interrupts the loop by helping a person contact feared or avoided triggers while refraining from compulsive responses. NIMH describes ERP as an effective treatment that exposes people to triggers and teaches them not to engage in their usual compulsions (National Institute of Mental Health, 2023). Clinical guidelines also support CBT that includes ERP as a central psychological treatment for OCD (National Institute for Health and Care Excellence, 2005).

The goal is not to prove that feared outcomes are impossible. That would turn treatment into a certainty service. The work is closer to learning that uncertainty, anxiety, disgust, or incompleteness can be experienced without the ritual that has been recruited to resolve it.

"Just Right" Can Still Be OCD

Not every OCD loop begins with a vivid catastrophe.

Some people repeat actions until they feel complete or "just right." They may reread a line, touch something again, rewrite a word, arrange an object, or repeat a movement because an internal sense of wrongness is difficult to leave unresolved.

This is one place where OCD and OCPD can look particularly similar.

The distinction cannot be reduced to "fear versus perfectionism." A person with OCD may appear extremely perfectionistic because they are chasing a feeling of certainty or completeness. A person with OCPD may appear ritualistic because they maintain detailed rules and standards.

Return to function.

For OCD, the repetition may be serving an urge to neutralize incompleteness or reduce obsessional distress. For OCPD, the repeated refinement may be serving a conviction that the work must meet a particular standard, often within a broader pattern of perfectionism and control.

The words someone uses are clues. The sequence is better evidence.

What Poor Insight Changes

Popular descriptions sometimes say that people with OCD "know their fears are irrational." That is too simple.

Many people with OCD do recognize that their fears or compulsions are excessive. Some are less sure. The DSM-5-TR includes insight specifiers for OCD, reflecting that people vary in how convinced they are about obsessional beliefs (American Psychiatric Association, 2022).

This matters for your Stance lens.

Suppose Nadia believes that a failure to perform a ritual could genuinely cause harm. Her conviction does not automatically make the pattern OCPD. You would still ask whether there are recurrent obsessions, compulsive responses, relief, avoidance, time cost, and impairment.

Conversely, someone who says, "I know I am too perfectionistic" does not automatically have OCD. Self-criticism is not the same as an unwanted obsession.

Insight modifies the picture. It does not replace the picture.

Avoidance Belongs in the Loop

An OCD pattern can be maintained by what a person does not do.

Someone afraid of contamination stops touching doorknobs. Someone afraid of violent thoughts avoids knives. Someone trapped in relationship doubt avoids saying "I love you" because the phrase triggers internal checking. Someone afraid of making mistakes delegates all financial tasks, not because they are flexible but because the responsibility feels intolerable.

Avoidance can make symptoms look quieter while life becomes smaller.

When you make a record, include avoided situations. "Nothing happened because I stayed home" may be a clinically important event.

The same caution applies to OCPD. A person may avoid delegating, not because the task is frightening in an obsessional sense, but because they cannot accept another person's method. Again, same visible choice, different possible function.

Do Not Turn Recognition Into Reassurance

Books about OCD can become part of OCD.

A reader may search a paragraph for proof that a disturbing thought is "really OCD." They may compare their symptoms with examples, feel relief, then return an hour later because the wording did not cover one detail.

If you notice that happening, treat it as information. This book cannot certify what a thought means.

A safer reading rule is: **use examples to generate questions, not verdicts**.

Instead of asking, "Does Sofia's story prove my violent thought is OCD?" write:

"My thought is intrusive and unwanted. I respond by reviewing my intentions for forty minutes. The review brings short-term relief. I want a clinician to assess whether that sequence is an OCD loop."

The second statement contains observations a professional can evaluate. It does not require the book to reassure you.

Build an OCD Loop Card

Choose one recurring episode and complete this card once.

Prompt	Your example
Trigger	
Intrusive thought, image, urge, or sense of wrongness	
What I feared it meant or could cause	
What I did next	
What changed immediately	
How long relief lasted	
What the pattern cost in time, energy, relationships, or opportunity	

If you cannot identify an obsession, do not invent one to make the form fit. Write "unclear." If the behavior seems driven more by a standard you endorse than by an intrusive threat, note that too.

The card is most useful when it preserves ambiguity.

A Useful Distinction for the Next Chapter

OCD can produce enormous efforts to control thoughts, feelings, risk, and uncertainty. So the word *control* alone does not distinguish OCD from OCPD.

In OCD, control efforts often serve an obsessional threat. In OCPD, control is more likely to appear as a broad, enduring way of organizing tasks, standards, people, and decisions.

Chapter 4 moves from the loop to that broader pattern.

What Happens When the Compulsion Is Delayed?

One way clinicians understand a possible compulsion is by examining what happens when the response is not immediately available.

You do not need to create an exposure experiment on your own. You can often use episodes that happened naturally.

Maybe you wanted to check a lock but were already on a train.

Maybe you wanted reassurance but your partner was asleep.

Maybe you wanted to review a memory but a meeting began.

What happened next?

Did anxiety rise? Did your mind generate arguments for why this time was different? Did you substitute another ritual, such as mental review or internet searching? Did the urge fade without the response? Did anger rather than fear become central?

These observations can show what the behavior has been regulating.

Write down natural interruptions when they occur. Do not deliberately create high-risk situations, and do not treat the outcome as proof of a diagnosis.

Compulsions Can Change Form

A person can stop one visible ritual and continue the same certainty project in a quieter form.

Repeated checking can become repeated photographing.

Questions to a partner can become online searches.

Out-loud confession can become mental review.

Avoidance can become elaborate planning that prevents contact with uncertainty.

This is why a treatment plan needs to identify the process rather than only one behavior.

If a visible ritual has reduced but the time spent seeking certainty has not, tell the clinician exactly what replaced it. That replacement may be more informative than the fact that the original ritual disappeared.

Chapter 4: The OCPD Pattern From Inside

A symptom can be episodic. A personality pattern is broader.

That is the central idea of the Reach lens.

OCPD is described as a persistent pattern involving order, perfectionism, and control that extends across contexts and affects functioning. Clinical descriptions include detail focus, perfectionism that can interfere with finishing tasks, excessive devotion to work, inflexibility, difficulty discarding items, reluctance to delegate unless others follow the preferred method, restrictive attitudes toward spending, and rigidity or stubbornness (Zimmerman, 2026; Pinto et al., 2022).

A list of features can help, but it does not show what living inside the pattern feels like.

For many people, the pattern is built around a sincere belief that standards matter.

When the Rule Feels Like the Responsible Position

Mei supervises six people.

She does not think of herself as controlling. She thinks of herself as the person who prevents avoidable mistakes. Her team has procedures because procedures reduce errors. She reviews work because quality matters. She rewrites sections because clients deserve accuracy.

Each statement can be true.

The problem appears when no amount of competence in other people earns flexibility. Mei gives instructions so detailed that a task takes longer to explain than to do. She rejects good work because it was produced by a different method. When deadlines slip, she interprets the delay as evidence that she needs more oversight rather than less.

The Reach lens asks whether the same organizing principle appears elsewhere. At home, Mei controls how bills are filed. On trips, she struggles when the itinerary changes. In volunteer work, she takes over because other people are "not serious enough." Arguments repeatedly end with the same conclusion: if others would simply do things properly, there would be no conflict.

That breadth matters.

OCPD is not a single preference for neatness. It is a pervasive pattern in which standards, productivity, details, rules, or control can become inflexible enough to create costs (Pinto et al., 2022).

Perfectionism Can Prevent Completion

The phrase *perfectionism* often sounds like a flattering weakness.

"I care too much."

"I have high standards."

"I just want things done right."

Clinical descriptions of OCPD point to a harsher version: perfectionism can interfere with task completion (American Psychiatric Association, 2022).

The distinction is easy to miss because the person may work constantly.

Theo spends twelve hours preparing a presentation that was expected to take three. He adjusts spacing, rewrites sentences, and researches points that are unlikely to affect the decision. He misses the internal deadline, then works overnight. When a colleague suggests sending the version they have, Theo is offended by the idea that "good enough" should be acceptable.

From the outside, this can look like dedication. The question is whether the standard helps the task serve its purpose or whether the task has become subordinate to the standard.

A useful observation is the **finish test**:

> *When the work has met the real requirement, what stops me from considering it finished?*

Possible answers differ.

"I get a recurring fear that a hidden error will cause harm, and I check to make the fear go away" points toward an OCD process worth assessing.

"I believe work should not leave my hands unless it meets my exact standard, even when the deadline and other people would be better served by stopping" points toward an OCPD-style perfectionistic pattern worth assessing.

Both can occur together.

Delegation Reveals More Than Workload

Difficulty delegating is particularly useful because it brings standards into a relationship.

A person may refuse to delegate for many reasons. Perhaps no one else is available. Perhaps the task is confidential. Perhaps the organization has punished mistakes. Perhaps anxiety makes responsibility hard to share.

In OCPD, the problem often concerns method. Another person can be capable and still feel unacceptable because they will not do the task in the prescribed way.

Try this question:

> *If the outcome would be competent and safe, how much difference in method can I tolerate?*

Do not judge the answer. Notice it.

Rafael asks his adult daughter to book a family rental. She finds a place within budget that meets everyone's stated needs. He spends the next evening rebuilding her comparison spreadsheet because she did not weight parking, cancellation terms, and walking distance the way he would. He tells himself that he is helping. She tells him she will not plan the next trip.

The cost is not in the spreadsheet. It is in the repeated message that another person's competent judgment does not count unless it resembles his own.

Work Can Become a Moral Measure

Clinical OCPD descriptions include excessive devotion to work and productivity at the expense of leisure and relationships when this is not explained by financial necessity (American Psychiatric Association, 2022).

The useful word is not *busy*. Many people are forced into punishing schedules by money, caregiving, discrimination, unstable work, or crisis.

The relevant pattern is the value assigned to productivity.

Aisha feels uneasy during unstructured time. Rest has to be earned. A weekend that produces nothing tangible feels wasted. She cancels social plans to finish tasks that are not urgent. When her partner asks for a day without work, Aisha hears the request as irresponsibility.

This is where a personality pattern differs from a temporary season of overwork. The question is not whether someone has had a busy month. It is whether productivity has become a rigid organizing value and whether that rigidity creates impairment.

Rules and Morality

OCPD can involve excessive conscientiousness and inflexibility around morality, ethics, or values, outside what would be expected from culture or religion (American Psychiatric Association, 2022).

This feature requires care. Strong values are not pathology. Religious observance is not pathology. Political conviction is not pathology. Cultural rules should not be measured against a clinician's personal preferences.

The issue is inflexibility, context, and impairment.

OCD can also involve morality, often called scrupulosity when obsessions and compulsions center on moral or religious fears. A person with OCD may be tormented by intrusive uncertainty about whether they sinned and repeatedly confess or seek reassurance. A person with an OCPD pattern may be rigidly convinced that a moral rule must be applied a particular way and may demand that others conform.

The content can sound almost identical. Trigger, Stance, Function, and Reach help separate them.

The Broad-Pattern Timeline

The Reach lens works best with time.

Create a simple timeline with four periods: late adolescence, early adulthood, the last five years, and now. If those periods do not fit your age, choose comparable spans.

For each period, ask about four domains:

Domain	Questions
Work or school	Did perfectionism, detail focus, control, or difficulty delegating repeatedly create delays or conflict?
Home	Were routines and standards flexible when circumstances changed?
Relationships	Did other people experience rules, correction, or control as a recurring problem?

Domain	Questions
Money and possessions	Were spending, saving, discarding, or keeping items governed by unusually rigid rules?

Do not use this as a memory test. Exact childhood reconstruction is difficult, and diagnostic assessment should not depend on a workbook's retrospective certainty.

The point is pattern recognition. If a behavior appeared only after a recent stressor, that is different information from a style visible across many years and settings.

The Strength Trap

Some OCPD features can be rewarded.

Precision can improve work. Persistence can build expertise. Conscientiousness can make someone reliable. Planning can prevent mistakes.

That does not mean OCPD is secretly a superpower, and it does not mean every driven person has a disorder.

The useful question is whether a strength remains flexible.

A rule that can adapt to context is a tool. A rule that repeatedly outranks deadlines, relationships, health, or reasonable alternatives may be controlling the person as much as the person is controlling the task.

The distinction is not "good trait versus bad trait." It is flexibility, reach, and cost.

A Pattern Without a Villain

OCPD is often discussed by frustrated partners, employees, or relatives. Their distress matters. So does the danger of turning a diagnosis into a character verdict.

Rigidity can hurt people without making the rigid person malicious.

The same principle applies to OCD. Reassurance seeking can exhaust a family without making the person with OCD manipulative.

This book will keep separating behavior from moral judgment because diagnostic clarity gets worse when everyone is defending their character.

For your record, add one question to each broad pattern you identify:

What does this pattern cost me or other people when circumstances require flexibility?

That cost, together with reach, is more informative than whether the trait sounds admirable.

Flexibility Is Easier to See Under Changing Conditions

A standard does not reveal much when the environment cooperates.

It becomes more informative when circumstances change.

Imagine a family trip with a cancelled flight, a work project with a shortened deadline, or a household week in which someone is ill. Most people have preferences. The question is what happens when reality makes the preferred method expensive.

Can the person lower a standard temporarily?

Can they accept another competent person's way?

Can they distinguish a safety requirement from a preference?

Can they tolerate a task being adequate rather than ideal?

A broad inability to adapt can make the cost of an OCPD pattern easier to see. It can also appear in autism, anxiety, trauma-related coping, and other contexts, so developmental and diagnostic history still matter.

Ask Whose Standard It Is

Standards can come from many places.

A law may require it.

A profession may require it.

A culture or faith community may value it.

A family may have taught it.

A person may have developed it privately.

When you record a rule, add its source if you know it.

Then ask whether the standard is being applied more rigidly than the context requires. The issue is not whether your clinician personally prefers a looser way of living. The issue is whether inflexibility is pervasive and costly in the context that actually governs your life.

That distinction is especially important when moral, religious, financial, or occupational rules are involved.

Chapter 5: The Insight Shortcut Has Limits

There is a sentence repeated in explanations of OCD and OCPD:

"OCD is ego-dystonic. OCPD is ego-syntonic."

It is memorable. It is useful. It is also too blunt to carry a diagnosis.

This chapter is about using it without being trapped by it.

What the Two Terms Actually Add

Ego-dystonic describes an experience that feels inconsistent with a person's wishes, identity, or values.

An intrusive thought about stabbing a loved one may feel alien and horrifying. A person does not want the thought and may spend enormous effort proving that it does not reflect who they are.

Ego-syntonic describes an experience that feels compatible with a person's values or self-concept.

A rule such as "A competent person should never submit work with avoidable imperfections" may feel not only familiar but correct. The person may defend it even when the cost is high.

Clinical descriptions commonly use this distinction when differentiating OCD from OCPD (Zimmerman, 2026).

The trouble begins when readers convert a tendency into a gate.

"If I think my rule is reasonable, I cannot have OCD."

"If I hate my perfectionism, I cannot have OCPD."

Neither conclusion is safe.

OCD Insight Exists on a Range

OCD is not defined by perfect awareness that the obsessional fear is unreasonable.

Some people recognize immediately that the feared consequence is unlikely. Others are uncertain. Some hold obsessional beliefs with high conviction. Diagnostic criteria explicitly account for variation in insight (American Psychiatric Association, 2022).

Jordan knows that a house fire is unlikely after the stove is off. He still feels compelled to photograph every burner before leaving.

Nadia is much less sure. After touching a public railing, she believes contamination probably will spread through her home unless she follows a washing sequence.

Their levels of conviction differ. Both patterns still require assessment in terms of obsessions, compulsions, distress, time, and impairment.

The question "Do you know this is irrational?" can therefore miss people.

A better set of questions is:

1. What happens if you resist the response?
2. What threat, meaning, or sense of wrongness appears?
3. Does performing the act bring short-term relief?
4. Does the doubt return and demand another response?

Those questions examine the loop.

OCPD Can Hurt From the Inside

The other half of the shortcut fails when people assume that ego-syntonic means pleasant.

A person can believe a standard is right and hate what it does to their life.

Marcus knows his marriage is strained by criticism. He has read enough to recognize his rigidity. He wishes arguments ended differently. Yet when his spouse says that towels do not need to be folded according to a fixed method, Marcus still thinks the method matters. His distress is largely about consequences and conflict, while the rule itself retains a sense of correctness.

That is different from an intrusive thought he wants removed from his mind.

But even this distinction is not pure. People can feel ambivalent about longstanding traits. Therapy, age, repeated consequences, depression, or relationship feedback can change how someone sees a pattern. A person who once defended every standard may now question it.

Stance is dynamic information.

Ask What You Would Keep

One of the most useful counterfactual questions is:

If the distress disappeared tomorrow, what part of this pattern would I still want to keep?

If Sofia's fear of harming someone disappeared, she would not want to keep three hours of mental review. The review has value only because it promises safety or certainty.

If Theo could avoid conflict and missed deadlines, he might still want to keep an unusually strict standard because he believes the standard produces better work.

That difference can be informative.

It is not foolproof. A person with OCD might value routines that have become entangled with compulsions. A person with OCPD may desperately want to become less rigid. A person with both can answer differently for different behaviors.

Use the question to generate a discussion, not a score.

Shame Distorts Stance

Shame can make an endorsed standard sound unwanted.

Suppose a person says, "I hate how controlling I am." You might hear ego-dystonicity.

Ask one more question: "When someone does the task differently, do you think their way is acceptable?"

If the answer is, "No. I hate that I have to police everyone, but they really are careless," the stance toward the consequences and the stance toward the standard are different.

The reverse can also happen in OCD. A person may defend a compulsion because admitting uncertainty feels too dangerous. "Of course I check the locks. Anyone sensible would." Further assessment may reveal a recurring intrusive fear, repeated checking far beyond ordinary safety behavior, and temporary relief.

A single self-description does not settle function.

An Insight Grid

Choose one behavior and separate four questions that are often collapsed.

Question	Your answer
Do I like having this pattern?	
Do I believe the underlying thought or rule is true or correct?	
Do I believe the behavior is necessary?	
Can I see costs even if I still defend the rule?	

Now add a fifth:

Question	Your answer
What happens emotionally if I do not follow it?	

The last answer is often where mechanism becomes visible.

Fear, guilt, disgust, or obsessional uncertainty may suggest an OCD process to assess. Anger at disorder, frustration with other people's methods, or a sense that standards are being violated may suggest an OCPD pattern to assess. Either set of reactions can occur in other conditions too.

Insight Is Not Intelligence

Another misconception is that people with better education or greater psychological knowledge should have better insight.

Insight is not an intelligence test.

A person can explain OCD in clinical language and still be unsure whether a specific fear is real. A person can understand OCPD intellectually and still defend a rule as necessary. Knowledge does not automatically dissolve conviction.

This is relevant to self-help because reading can produce an illusion of certainty. You learn the vocabulary, then start using the vocabulary as proof.

Try not to.

The purpose of terms such as ego-dystonic and ego-syntonic is to describe experience precisely enough to be examined. Their job is not to let the reader close the case.

What to Say Instead of "I Have Insight"

Clinicians usually learn more from examples than from labels.

Instead of:

"I have good insight."

Try:

"I know the probability is low, but I still feel that I need to check until I am certain."

Instead of:

"My perfectionism is ego-syntonic."

Try:

"I dislike the conflict it causes, but I still believe my standard is the responsible standard and I get angry when people ask me to lower it."

Instead of:

"My thoughts are ego-dystonic."

Try:

"The thought arrives against my wishes, and I spend time trying to prove it does not reflect what I want."

Those sentences preserve the distinction without pretending it is binary.

The Rule for the Rest of the Book

Use stance as one lens among five.

A good differential formulation should survive even if the answer to "Does this feel like me?" is complicated.

The next chapter applies that principle to one of the hardest practical problems: the same visible behavior can do a completely different job in two people.

Stance Can Change During One Episode

Do not assume your relationship to a thought or rule stays constant.

At the start of an OCD episode, you may believe a feared outcome is quite plausible. After checking, you may see the fear as exaggerated. Ten minutes later, doubt may rise again.

With a rigid standard, you may defend the rule during conflict and question it later when you see the relational cost.

If you record stance, note the time.

"In the moment I was 90 percent convinced."

"Afterward I could see another explanation."

"I still think the rule is correct, but I regret how I enforced it."

This time-sensitive description is more useful than a permanent identity statement such as "I have insight."

Distinguish Conviction From Preference

"I prefer it this way" and "it must be this way" are not the same sentence.

Neither is "I fear what will happen if it is not this way."

Try finishing each of these:

"I prefer ..."

"I believe ..."

"I fear ..."

"I require ..."

"I wish I could stop ..."

"I wish other people would ..."

The answers may overlap, but they reveal different dimensions of stance. A person can prefer order, believe a rule is correct, fear a catastrophe, and wish to stop a ritual all in the same life.

That is why the Five-Lens Difference Map was built with more than one lens.

Chapter 6: Same Behavior, Different Job

If you remember one sentence from this book, let it be this:

Same behavior does not mean same function.

This chapter puts that rule under pressure.

We will compare checking, cleaning, arranging, list-making, reassurance, overpreparing, and correction. The purpose is not to assign each behavior to one diagnosis. It is to show why surface matching fails.

Checking

Lucas checks a contract six times.

In one version, a thought keeps returning: "What if I typed the wrong account number and destroy the transaction?" He checks, feels relief, then doubts whether he checked carefully enough. The act is caught in a repetitive certainty loop.

In another version, Lucas has a standard that every important document should be reviewed according to a detailed protocol. He becomes irritated when coworkers do not follow it. He may check far beyond what the task requires because he believes careful professionals should work that way.

In a third version, Lucas is new to a job where an error could have serious consequences and the organization requires multiple checks.

The number six does not diagnose anything.

Useful questions:

Lens	Checking questions
Trigger	What made checking feel necessary this time?
Stance	Was the concern intrusive and unwanted, or did the procedure feel correct and justified?
Function	Did checking reduce fear, or restore a preferred standard or sense of control?
Reach	Does similar overcontrol appear broadly outside the feared topic?
Treatment Fit	Has treatment targeted compulsive checking, rigid standards, or something else?

Cleaning and Order

Order is one of the most misleading stereotypes around OCD.

A person with contamination OCD may clean to reduce fear of illness, disgust, or responsibility for spreading contamination. The cleaning may be exhausting and unwanted.

A person with symmetry or "just right" OCD may arrange objects until an internal sense of wrongness resolves.

A person with OCPD may enforce order because order is a valued standard. Disorder itself may be experienced as careless, inefficient, or unacceptable.

A person with no disorder may simply like a tidy home.

Ask what happens when the environment remains imperfect.

Does the person fear a specific consequence? Do they feel an intolerable sense of incompleteness? Do they judge the situation as objectively improper? Do they become angry that another person violated a standard? Can they flex when the cost of order becomes larger than the benefit?

Those details matter more than whether the books are alphabetized.

Lists

A list can be a memory aid, a compulsion, a control system, or all three.

Priya writes a grocery list. Nothing clinically interesting follows.

Ben writes the same to-do list repeatedly because he fears that an omitted task will lead to catastrophe. Rewriting briefly reduces anxiety.

Elena builds a project list with dozens of substeps and requires everyone to follow it. The team loses time maintaining the system, but she believes deviation is evidence of carelessness.

The object is the same. The function differs.

For any repeated list-making, ask: "What would happen if I used a shorter list written once?"

Do not perform the experiment if your clinician has advised a different plan or if the task carries real safety consequences. As a reflection question, however, it can reveal whether the feared outcome is obsessional uncertainty, loss of control, ordinary forgetfulness, or something else.

Reassurance and Correction

OCD often recruits other people into the cycle through reassurance.

"Do you think I offended her?"

"Are you sure this mark is not a symptom?"

"Did you see me lock the door?"

The answer may calm the person briefly, but certainty does not last. Family accommodation can maintain OCD by helping rituals or avoidance continue, which is why OCD treatment often addresses reassurance patterns as part of the larger cycle (American Psychiatric Association, n.d.).

OCPD can also create repetitive interpersonal exchanges, but the function may be correction rather than reassurance.

"You need to redo that."

"That is not the right way to store it."

"If you followed the system, this would not happen."

The speaker may not be asking the other person to reduce an intrusive fear. They may be enforcing a standard.

Partners often experience both patterns as exhausting. The distinction matters because the helpful response may differ.

Overpreparing

Overpreparing can hide almost anywhere.

Maya rehearses a two-minute work introduction for three hours.

If she is driven by an intrusive fear that one imperfect phrase will prove she is incompetent and she repeatedly rehearses to neutralize doubt, an OCD process may be relevant.

If she is driven by a broad conviction that anything less than an optimized performance is unacceptable, and the same perfectionistic standard appears across tasks and relationships, OCPD features may be relevant.

If she has social anxiety and fears negative evaluation, another formulation may fit better.

If she is autistic and scripting reduces uncertainty in social communication, the context changes again.

This is why a differential guide must keep saying "both or neither." OCD and OCPD are not the only explanations for repetitive or rigid behavior.

Hoarding-Like Behavior

OCPD criteria have historically included difficulty discarding worn-out or worthless objects even without sentimental value. Hoarding disorder, however, is a separate condition with its own diagnostic features, and ordinary saving behavior has many causes (American Psychiatric Association, 2022).

Do not infer OCPD from a cluttered garage.

Ask about the reason for saving, the degree of difficulty discarding, the broader pattern, and whether other diagnostic possibilities have been assessed.

This book's role is not to perform every differential. Its role is to keep the OCPD/OCD question from crowding out context.

The Behavior Function Matrix

Choose up to three behaviors that create the most cost. Do not choose ten. More data is not automatically better data.

Behavior	Trigger	Immediate feared or valued issue	Response	Immediate effect	Broader pattern?
Example: reread sent email	Doubt after sending	Fear of harmful error	Reopen four times	Anxiety falls briefly	Mostly around responsibility fears
Example: redo colleague's file	Different method	Standard feels violated	Reformat personally	Control restored	Similar across work and home
Your behavior 1					
Your behavior 2					

Behavior	Trigger	Immedia te feared or valued issue	Response	Immedia te effect	Broader pattern?
Your behavior 3					

Now circle, mentally rather than literally, the column that contains the most useful information. It is rarely the first one.

The behavior name is the least specific part of the row.

Mixed Functions Are Real

A behavior can start with one function and acquire another.

Suppose Daniel checks a report because of obsessional doubt. Years of being praised for meticulous work may strengthen a broader identity around never making mistakes. He may begin to defend checking as a professional standard even when the original fear is quiet.

Or a person with longstanding OCPD traits may develop an OCD theme around responsibility. The broad rigidity was there first, then a specific obsession-compulsion loop formed inside it.

Mixed functions are one reason self-diagnosis by checklist performs poorly.

If you find two functions, write two functions. Do not choose the one that makes the story cleaner.

When the Function Is "I Don't Know"

Sometimes the most accurate answer is "I do not know."

You may notice the behavior only after it has been happening for twenty minutes. The emotion may be mixed. A rule may feel both correct and frightening to violate. The act may bring both anxiety relief and a restored sense of order.

Uncertainty does not make the exercise useless.

Bring one ambiguous example to a clinician and ask them to help formulate the sequence. The quality of the question is more important than the confidence of your provisional answer.

Run the "Different Person, Same Behavior" Test

When you are convinced that a behavior belongs to one diagnosis, imagine three people doing the same thing.

One is responding to intrusive fear.

One is enforcing a standard they believe is right.

One is responding to a real external requirement.

What would you need to know to tell them apart?

This thought exercise loosens the habit of diagnosing from appearance.

Take "checking the stove."

Person one checks because a fire image returns and checking buys temporary relief.

Person two checks as part of a household procedure and criticizes anyone who does not follow the exact sequence.

Person three is a restaurant manager completing a required closing safety checklist.

The action does not carry its own diagnosis.

Find the Stop Rule

Every repetitive behavior has some condition under which it stops.

For an OCD compulsion, the stop rule may be unstable: "when I feel certain," "when it feels right," or "when the anxiety is low enough." Because certainty or rightness does not hold, the behavior can restart.

For a perfectionistic standard, the stop rule may be a quality threshold: "when it meets my standard." The problem can be that the standard is inflexible, unrealistic, or applied where it is not needed.

For ordinary work, the stop rule may be objective: "when the required fields are complete."

Write the stop rule for one costly behavior.

If the answer is "I do not know when I am allowed to stop," that is worth bringing to treatment.

Chapter 7: When Perfectionism Is the Clue

Perfectionism sits in the overlap because it can describe a personality style, a coping strategy, a symptom-maintaining process, or an ordinary preference for high standards.

So "I am a perfectionist" is not a differential diagnosis.

The useful questions are: perfect for what, perfect according to whom, what happens when perfect is impossible, and how much of life is organized around the demand?

Perfectionism in OCPD

OCPD is strongly associated with maladaptive perfectionism, detail focus, control, and rigidity. One diagnostically relevant feature is perfectionism that interferes with completion of tasks (Pinto et al., 2022).

That last phrase separates clinical cost from a flattering self-description.

Rafael is preparing a budget for a volunteer organization. The board needs a clear estimate by Friday. He has enough information on Wednesday. He spends Thursday rebuilding assumptions that will not change the decision, then misses Friday because he wants to correct a small discrepancy.

When others say the budget was good enough, he hears lowered standards.

The key feature is not that he likes accuracy. It is that the pursuit of the standard defeats the actual purpose of the work.

Perfectionism in OCD

OCD can also produce intense perfectionistic behavior.

A person may need to know that a sentence is exactly right because an error feels morally dangerous. They may repeat an action until it feels complete. They may check work because uncertainty is intolerable. They may seek perfect certainty about a relationship, a memory, a health symptom, or a past decision.

Here, perfectionistic action can function as a compulsion.

Mei rereads a condolence message for ninety minutes. She is not trying to produce elegant prose. She is afraid that one wrong word will reveal that she is cruel. Each revision temporarily lowers guilt, then a new possible interpretation appears.

That is different from refining a message because she believes there is one objectively proper way to write it and that anyone who accepts less is careless.

Again, same behavior, different job.

The "Good Enough" Question

The phrase *good enough* is useful because it tests flexibility.

Ask:

> *If the task meets its real purpose, what makes stopping difficult?*

Four broad answers often appear:

1. "I fear a specific consequence, and checking reduces the fear."
2. "It still feels incomplete or wrong unless I repeat it."
3. "I believe the standard itself should not be lowered."
4. "I do not know. I just feel unable to stop."

The first two can occur in OCD. The third can fit an OCPD pattern. The fourth needs exploration.

But context matters. In surgery, aviation, engineering, finance, or other high-stakes work, "good enough" is defined by professional standards rather than convenience. A conscientious person may appropriately refuse a shortcut.

Clinical perfectionism is not diagnosed by asking whether someone cares more than their coworkers.

Standards Versus Threats

One way to distinguish two perfectionistic sequences is to listen for the sentence after "because."

"I have to reread it because if I made a mistake, something terrible could happen and I would be responsible."

"I have to reread it because a competent person should not allow mistakes that could be found."

These sentences can overlap, but they emphasize different processes.

The first is threat-centered.

The second is standard-centered.

Now ask what happens if a trusted authority says the work is acceptable.

In an OCD loop, reassurance may reduce anxiety briefly and then lose its effect. New doubts appear.

In an OCPD pattern, the person may reject the authority's standard as too lax. The problem is not lack of information. It is disagreement about what standard is correct.

That contrast is often revealing.

Perfectionism and Identity

OCPD-style perfectionism can become part of identity.

"I am the one who does things properly."

"I do not cut corners."

"Other people settle."

This identity can produce pride and reliability. It can also make flexibility feel like a character failure.

OCD perfectionism can become identity-laden too, especially when obsessions attach to morality or responsibility. The person may think, "A good person would make absolutely sure."

So identity language is not enough. The question remains whether the process is organized around intrusive obsessional threat and neutralization, a broad system of standards and control, or both.

Cost Accounting

Perfectionism often survives because its benefits are visible and its costs are scattered.

Create two columns for one standard.

What this standard gives me	What this standard costs
Accuracy	Time beyond what the task requires
Predictability	Difficulty delegating

What this standard gives me	What this standard costs
Pride in work	Missed deadlines
Reduced uncertainty	Repeated checking or reassurance
Order	Conflict when others use a different method

Do not use the balance to decide whether you "should" have the standard. Use it to make impairment concrete.

A clinician needs to know not only that you are perfectionistic, but whether the pattern consumes time, prevents completion, damages relationships, narrows life, or produces significant distress.

Perfectionism Without OCPD or OCD

This chapter would be misleading if it implied that perfectionism belongs to two diagnoses.

It does not.

Perfectionism is transdiagnostic. It appears in many psychological problems and can exist as a trait without a disorder. A clinician may need to consider anxiety, depression, eating disorders, neurodevelopmental differences, trauma-related coping, personality traits, cultural pressures, occupational demands, and other explanations.

The Five-Lens Difference Map can still help because it forces the question back to process and context.

If your answer does not fit either column in this book, do not squeeze it in.

A Perfectionism Autopsy

Choose one recent task that took too long.

Answer these questions once:

Question	Notes
What was the task's actual requirement?	
At what point was that requirement met?	
What did I continue doing after that point?	

Question	Notes
What did I believe would happen if I stopped?	
Was the problem fear, incompleteness, standards, control, shame, or something else?	
Would I have accepted the same quality if another competent person produced it?	
What did the extra effort cost?	

Bring the completed example to the next chapter if relationships are where perfectionism becomes most visible. Other people often see reach before the person living inside the pattern does.

The Standard Ladder

One way to make perfectionism visible is to rank the real stakes of tasks.

Choose three recent tasks.

One should be low stakes, such as choosing a font for a private note.

One should be moderate stakes, such as sending a routine work email.

One should be genuinely high stakes, such as a decision with meaningful financial, health, legal, or safety consequences.

Now compare the amount of checking, revision, and control you used.

Flexible standards usually change with stakes.

If every task receives the same maximal treatment, ask why.

An OCD process may flatten stakes because uncertainty itself feels threatening. An OCPD pattern may flatten stakes because the standard is experienced as a principle that should not be lowered. Other explanations are possible.

The point is to see whether effort follows reality.

Perfectionism Between People

Perfectionism becomes especially informative when someone else completes the task adequately.

If you can recognize that their method differs and leave it alone, your standard has some flexibility.

If you have to redo the work to reduce fear, note the feared consequence and relief.

If you have to redo the work because accepting their method feels like endorsing poor standards, note that stance.

If you are simply annoyed but choose not to intervene, note that too.

The ability to experience discomfort without forcing the environment to conform is useful information across several formulations.

Chapter 8: What Partners Usually See

Partners rarely meet a diagnosis first. They meet a pattern.

They meet the fourth request for reassurance before leaving the house. They meet the argument about how a cupboard should be organized. They meet the hour lost to checking, the plan that cannot change, the repeated correction, the refusal to let someone else finish a task.

From the outside, OCD and OCPD can both look controlling.

That word is emotionally understandable and diagnostically imprecise.

This chapter gives partners a better vocabulary.

Impact Is Real Even When Function Differs

A partner does not have to know the correct diagnosis before naming an impact.

If reassurance takes over evenings, the impact is real.

If every household task is governed by one person's method, the impact is real.

If plans cannot change because uncertainty triggers rituals, the impact is real.

If plans cannot change because deviation is treated as irresponsible, the impact is real.

The distinction matters for treatment, but it does not erase the burden on the household.

That is important because partners sometimes get trapped in a false choice: either show compassion for a mental health problem or insist that the behavior affecting them must change. Those are not mutually exclusive positions.

You can understand function and still set limits.

Reassurance in OCD

OCD can recruit partners into compulsions.

Aisha asks her partner whether she locked the door. He says yes. She asks whether he saw her pull the handle. He says yes. She asks whether the latch looked fully engaged. By the fourth question, he is irritated. Aisha hears irritation as evidence that he was not paying attention and asks again.

From Aisha's side, each question is an attempt to get enough certainty to leave.

From her partner's side, the evening is now organized around a question he cannot answer with the degree of certainty OCD demands.

Family accommodation is clinically relevant in OCD. Repeated reassurance, helping with rituals, or modifying family routines around symptoms can maintain the cycle, which is why treatment plans may include guidance for family members about how to respond (American Psychiatric Association, n.d.).

That does not mean a partner should abruptly refuse all reassurance based on a paragraph in a book. Changes in accommodation are best coordinated with the person's treatment plan, especially when symptoms are severe.

The useful observation is the sequence:

reassurance request, answer, temporary relief, renewed doubt, another request.

That sequence is stronger evidence than the accusation "You never trust me."

Correction and Standards in OCPD

An OCPD pattern can create a different relational sequence.

Daniel watches his partner load groceries into the refrigerator. He moves the yogurt to another shelf. His partner moves it back. Daniel explains that the refrigerator works more efficiently when categories stay consistent. His partner says she wants to put away groceries without being supervised.

Daniel is not asking for reassurance. He is asserting a standard.

If the pattern is broad, the same structure may show up in finances, cleaning, parenting, driving, travel, and time management. The partner experiences the relationship as full of micro-corrections. The person with OCPD traits may experience the same moments as repeated encounters with avoidable disorder.

The question is not who wins the yogurt argument.

The question is whether one person's rules have become so inflexible that the other person's ordinary agency is repeatedly overridden.

Do Not Diagnose Your Partner From This Book

Partner readers have a special risk: a comparison table can become courtroom evidence.

"You are clearly OCPD."

"See, this says your need for control is pathological."

That use is likely to make both the relationship and the assessment worse.

A diagnosis requires evaluation of the person, including history, functioning, context, other possible explanations, and the person's own experience. You can observe behavior. You can name impact. You can request change. You cannot complete a valid psychiatric assessment of someone who is not participating.

Replace labels with specific descriptions.

Instead of:

"Your OCPD ruins every trip."

Try:

"When the itinerary changes, we often spend an hour arguing about restoring the plan. I want us to find a way to make travel decisions that does not give one person total control."

Instead of:

"Your OCD is making me crazy."

Try:

"We have answered the same safety question six times tonight. I can see that you are distressed, and I do not think more answers are helping. I would like us to follow the plan you and your therapist made for reassurance."

The first sentence in each pair invites a diagnosis fight. The second describes an observable problem.

The Partner's Five Lenses

A partner can use the Five-Lens Difference Map without claiming access to another person's mind.

Lens	What a partner can observe	What a partner cannot know without asking
Trigger	What happened before the behavior	The exact thought or meaning
Stance	Whether the person defends or resists the behavior	The full internal experience

Lens	What a partner can observe	What a partner cannot know without asking
Function	What seems to change afterward	The complete reason for the behavior
Reach	Settings, duration, repeated relationship patterns	Hidden symptoms or private rituals
Treatment Fit	What the treatment plan is meant to address, if shared	Whether a diagnosis is correct

Notice the boundary in the last column.

Partners can provide excellent collateral information. They often notice reach, frequency, and interpersonal cost. But observation should be offered as information, not as a verdict.

The "Who Has to Change?" Test

One relational clue worth recording is where flexibility is expected.

In an OCD loop, the person may ask others to help make uncertainty disappear: answer again, check again, avoid the trigger, clean differently, promise safety.

In an OCPD pattern, the person may ask others to conform to a standard: do the task my way, spend according to my rule, follow my schedule, organize the environment correctly.

Both can become controlling from the partner's perspective.

Ask:

What change is being demanded of the other person, and what problem is that change supposed to solve?

This question often exposes function.

If the requested change is meant to eliminate uncertainty or prevent an obsessional threat, OCD may be relevant.

If the requested change is meant to enforce a preferred standard across ordinary life, OCPD may be relevant.

If it is about coercion, intimidation, abuse, or safety, the diagnostic label is not the first problem to solve. Mental health terminology should never be used to excuse abusive behavior.

Boundaries Are Not Differential Tests

A boundary tells another person what you will do. It does not diagnose why they behave as they do.

Examples:

"I will discuss the budget for thirty minutes. If we cannot agree, we will schedule another time rather than continue until one of us gives in."

"I will not repeatedly confirm whether the stove is off. If this is part of your OCD plan, I will use the response we agreed with your clinician."

"I am willing to share household tasks. I am not willing to have completed tasks redone in front of me because my method differs."

"I will not participate in arguments where I am insulted or threatened. I will leave the conversation and return only when it is safe."

Boundaries do not require diagnostic certainty.

This is particularly useful for partners who have spent months researching labels because they think they need the right label before they are allowed to object to a pattern.

You do not.

A Two-Person Observation Sheet

If both people agree, choose one recurring conflict and write separately before comparing.

Prompt	Person A	Person B
What happened immediately before the conflict?		
What did I think needed to happen?		
What did I fear or believe would happen if it did not?		
What did I ask the other person to do?		
What happened after they complied or refused?		

Prompt	Person A	Person B
Is this pattern specific or broad across our relationship?		

The purpose is not to catch inconsistencies. Two people can accurately describe different parts of the same event.

If the exercise becomes a debate about whose account is "correct," stop. That result is itself information about the relationship, but the worksheet will not settle it.

When a Partner Should Be in the Clinical Conversation

With the patient's consent, a partner can sometimes help a clinician understand frequency, accommodation, interpersonal effects, and patterns that are hard to recall in the room.

A partner might say:

"I am not trying to assign a diagnosis. I notice two different patterns. One involves repeated reassurance after intrusive fears. The other is a broad pattern of rules about tasks and finances that he usually defends as correct. Could both be relevant to the formulation?"

That is useful collateral information.

It is also respectful of the clinician's role.

The next chapter moves into another setting where strengths and symptoms can hide each other: work.

A Partner Can Track the Loop Without Naming It

If both people agree, a partner can keep a short log for one week.

Do not record personality judgments.

Record requests and outcomes.

"Asked whether the door was locked four times. Each answer calmed him for a few minutes."

"Asked me to redo the grocery list because I used a different category system. She defended the system as the only sensible one."

"Wanted to cancel dinner because of a contamination fear."

"Corrected the route I chose despite identical arrival time."

These notes can help a clinician see frequency and Reach.

They can also reveal where the partner is becoming part of the pattern.

Compassion Does Not Require Unlimited Participation

Partners sometimes fear that any limit is unkind.

Limits can be part of responsible care.

The exact limit depends on the behavior, safety, treatment plan, and relationship. A partner should not improvise a complex ERP program from a book. They can still say what they will and will not participate in.

The most useful boundary language is behavioral.

"I will not answer the same question ten times."

"I will not give up responsibility for every household task because my method differs."

"I will follow the safety plan we agreed."

"I will leave a conversation if I am being threatened."

A diagnosis may explain why a pattern is difficult to change. It does not erase the other person's right to safety and agency.

Chapter 9: What Work Can Hide

Workplaces reward many behaviors that can make differential diagnosis harder.

Accuracy is rewarded. Reliability is rewarded. Planning is rewarded. Persistence is rewarded. In some roles, checking is required. In others, a person who never delegates may be praised for "ownership" until the team stops functioning.

A pattern can therefore produce promotions before it produces a crisis.

The workplace is useful not because it reveals a diagnosis, but because it makes function and cost visible under deadlines, hierarchy, and shared responsibility.

When Checking Looks Like Quality Control

Marcus is an analyst. Every report goes through a formal quality check.

That is ordinary process.

What happens after the required check is where the Five-Lens Difference Map begins.

Marcus may reopen the report five more times because a doubt keeps returning: "What if I missed a number that will cause a client loss?" Each check brings temporary relief. He knows the report passed review, but the knowledge will not hold. That can resemble an OCD checking loop.

Or Marcus may redo the team's approved review because he believes the official standard is too lax. He is less interested in eliminating a specific intrusive fear than in making the product meet his own stricter standard. He becomes frustrated when colleagues ask him to stop. That may fit an OCPD pattern.

Or the organization may truly have poor controls and Marcus is compensating for a real risk.

Context prevents pathologizing competence.

The Deadline Test

Deadlines create a natural conflict between perfection and purpose.

A task usually has at least three constraints: quality, time, and resources.

Healthy flexibility means the standard can respond to the actual stakes. A draft internal memo does not need the same polish as a regulatory filing. A prototype does not need the same finish as a released product.

OCPD-style perfectionism can flatten those distinctions. Every task starts to feel as though it deserves the highest available standard.

OCD can also cause missed deadlines, but the path may look different. Time disappears into checking, reviewing, neutralizing, reassurance, or avoidance driven by obsessional doubt.

Record not only that you missed the deadline, but why the extra hour felt necessary.

Extra work	What made stopping difficult?	Immediate effect of continuing
Rechecked calculations	Fear of causing harm through error	Anxiety fell briefly
Reformatted slides	Belief that inconsistent spacing is unprofessional	Felt that quality was restored
Rewrote email	Needed wording to feel morally safe	Guilt fell briefly
Took task back from colleague	Belief that only my method met the standard	Regained control

The third column is often more revealing than the first.

Delegation Is an Assessment Opportunity

Delegation requires tolerating two things: another person's judgment and some loss of direct control.

That makes it useful for identifying a broad OCPD pattern.

Suppose your colleague is competent, understands the goal, and meets the actual standard. Can you allow a different method?

If not, ask what feels wrong.

"I worry that if I am not personally responsible, I will not know whether a hidden mistake caused harm" may point toward obsessional responsibility.

"Their method is inefficient and I cannot accept putting my name on work done that way" may point toward standards and control.

"I am afraid they will outperform me and I will lose status" points somewhere else.

The same refusal to delegate can have several functions.

High Performance Does Not Cancel Impairment

People sometimes assume that a successful career rules out a personality disorder or severe OCD.

It does not.

Mental health impairment is not measured only by whether someone is employed. A person can be highly skilled and still lose enormous time to rituals. They can be promoted and still create severe team conflict. They can earn well and still sacrifice health, relationships, or sustainable functioning to rigid productivity.

The Reach lens should therefore include invisible costs.

Ask:

How many hours are required for work other people complete in less time?

How much work is redone after it already meets the requirement?

How often do colleagues avoid asking for help because they expect correction?

How much distress occurs when someone else controls the process?

What parts of life are repeatedly sacrificed to work that is not financially necessary or truly urgent?

These questions are about functioning, not moral worth.

The Manager Problem

A person with strong OCPD traits can sometimes thrive as an individual contributor and struggle after promotion.

As an individual contributor, meticulousness may produce excellent output.

As a manager, the same standards must pass through other people.

Elena gives her team detailed instructions. When they bring back good work in a different format, she corrects it. Soon, staff stop making decisions without approval. Elena experiences their dependence as proof that they need more supervision.

This can become a self-reinforcing system.

The team loses initiative because initiative is corrected. The manager sees less initiative and increases control.

That interpersonal feedback loop is different from the OCD relief loop, although a person can experience both.

If this pattern sounds familiar, note how other people's behavior changes around you. Reach includes what a pattern elicits from the environment.

The Quiet Employee with OCD

OCD can be nearly invisible at work.

Aisha arrives early because she needs time to perform a checking sequence before anyone notices. She keeps dozens of draft emails because deleting them triggers doubt. During meetings, she mentally reviews whether she sounded offensive. She seems conscientious and calm.

The cost appears after hours.

She stays late to repeat work. She avoids promotions that would increase responsibility. She spends weekends replaying decisions.

A workplace observer might call her perfectionistic. The internal function tells a different story.

This is why third-party impressions have limits.

Reasonable Accommodation and Professional Help

If symptoms or personality patterns significantly affect work, a qualified clinician can help with assessment and treatment. Workplace accommodations may also be relevant depending on the situation, employer, role, and applicable law.

This book cannot give employment-law advice. It also cannot decide which workplace adjustment is clinically appropriate.

What it can do is help you prepare a functional description:

"I lose about ninety minutes a day reopening completed work because of recurrent doubts about having caused harm through mistakes."

"I repeatedly take tasks back from competent staff because I cannot tolerate different methods, which is causing missed deadlines and conflict."

Those descriptions are more actionable than "I am obsessive at work."

The Work Pattern Audit

Choose one ordinary workweek. Estimate conservatively rather than trying to produce a perfect measurement.

Pattern	Frequency or time	What drives it?	Cost
Rechecking completed work			
Redoing others' work			
Avoiding decisions			
Difficulty stopping			
Reassurance or approval seeking			
Conflict over methods			

Now ask whether the pattern exists outside work.

If it appears only in one unusually demanding job, that context matters. If the same structure appears in money, travel, household tasks, parenting, and leisure, Reach changes.

Work is not proof. It is another window.

Compare Private Cost With Public Output

Workplaces often see the finished product, not the process that produced it.

A polished report can hide three hours of repeated checking.

An orderly team can hide staff who have stopped making independent decisions.

A reliable employee can hide weekends lost to rituals or perfectionistic overwork.

For one week, record both output and private cost.

"Report delivered on time" is the output.

"Started two hours early because I needed time for checking" is the cost.

"Project had no errors" is the output.

"Redid three colleagues' sections and stayed until midnight" is the cost.

This protects against the assumption that high performance means there is no impairment.

Ask What Happens to the Team

Some patterns change other people's behavior.

Coworkers may stop volunteering ideas because they expect correction.

Staff may wait for approval on minor decisions because independent choices are usually reversed.

A partner in a family business may take over reassurance because it seems faster than watching distress rise.

These environmental adaptations can make the original pattern look functional.

If everyone works around one person's rigidity or rituals, include that in the Reach lens. The system around the symptom can hide its cost.

Chapter 10: Both Can Be True

The word *versus* is useful in a title because it names the reader's question.

It can become misleading if it implies that the answer must be one or the other.

OCD and OCPD are distinct conditions, but they can co-occur. Reviews of the clinical literature discuss meaningful rates of co-occurring OCPD among people with OCD and the possibility that comorbidity can affect presentation and treatment complexity (Wheaton et al., 2022).

That means the Five-Lens Difference Map sometimes produces two patterns instead of one.

Two Patterns in One Person

Return to Maya.

Pattern one: she gets intrusive images of causing a kitchen fire. She checks the stove repeatedly, photographs the knobs, and sometimes returns home to inspect them. Checking reduces fear for a short time, then doubt returns.

Pattern two: she maintains strict household systems and insists that family members follow them. She rewrites shared calendars, controls how money is categorized, and has difficulty accepting "good enough" work from others. She usually believes these standards are sensible, though she sees the conflict they create.

If you force every behavior into one diagnosis, you lose information.

An OCD-only formulation might explain the stove checking well and struggle with pervasive interpersonal control.

An OCPD-only formulation might explain broad rigidity and struggle with the intrusive fire images and compulsive checking loop.

A clinician can assess whether both conditions, subthreshold traits, or another combination better explains the full picture.

Comorbidity Is Not a Failure of Diagnosis

People often want one elegant answer.

Medicine and psychology frequently do not work that way. Conditions can coexist. One can increase the burden of another. A symptom can belong to one process in one context and a different process elsewhere.

The job of diagnosis is not to produce the smallest possible number of labels. It is to produce a formulation that accounts for clinically meaningful patterns and helps guide care.

This matters because a person with two processes may need treatment to distinguish them explicitly.

An ERP task designed for an OCD compulsion has a clear target: the obsessional trigger and ritualized response.

Work on OCPD-related rigidity may focus on patterns such as inflexible standards, perfectionism, control, interpersonal consequences, and behavioral flexibility. The evidence base is smaller and treatment should be individualized (Pinto et al., 2022).

A combined case should not be treated as though every rigid behavior is a compulsion.

The Double-Count Problem

Checklists can accidentally count the same behavior twice.

Suppose someone spends three hours editing a report.

An OCD checklist might count repeated checking.

An OCPD checklist might count perfectionism interfering with completion.

Both descriptions may be true at the behavior level. The question is whether two distinct processes are present.

Ask:

If the obsessional fear were removed, would the perfectionistic overwork remain?

Then ask the reverse:

If I became more flexible about standards, would the intrusive fear and compulsion remain?

These counterfactuals cannot prove comorbidity. They can reveal whether one explanation seems insufficient.

Traits, Symptoms, and Disorders

Another source of confusion is the difference between a trait and a diagnosis.

Someone can have OCPD traits without meeting full diagnostic criteria. Someone can have obsessive-compulsive symptoms without meeting full criteria for OCD. Severity can change over time.

This matters because readers sometimes make the differential question unnecessarily absolute.

"I clearly have difficulty delegating, so I have OCPD."

That does not follow.

"I have intrusive thoughts, so I have OCD."

That does not follow either.

Diagnosis asks about the full pattern, thresholds, impairment, duration, and alternative explanations. This book intentionally stays at the level of observation.

The most accurate conclusion may be:

"I have an OCD diagnosis, and I also have longstanding perfectionistic and controlling traits that I want assessed."

That sentence can open useful clinical work without requiring you to pre-decide whether those traits add up to OCPD.

When One Pattern Hides the Other

OCD can make OCPD traits look like more OCD.

If a person already has an OCD diagnosis, clinicians and family members may interpret every repetitive or rigid behavior through that frame. A longstanding refusal to delegate can be assumed to be a compulsion even when no obsessional loop is evident.

The reverse can happen too.

If someone is known as rigid and perfectionistic, intrusive obsessions may be dismissed as "overthinking" or another expression of control. Hidden mental compulsions can remain unrecognized.

A good differential review asks the same questions about each costly behavior rather than assuming the first diagnosis owns all of them.

A Two-Column Formulation

If you suspect two processes, build two provisional columns.

Pattern A: possible obsession-compulsion loop	Pattern B: possible broad standards/control pattern
Intrusive trigger:	Longstanding rule or standard:
Compulsive response:	Control/perfectionistic response:
Short-term relief:	Short-term restoration of order/control:
Main settings:	Main settings:
Costs:	Costs:
Questions for clinician:	Questions for clinician:

Do not label the columns "OCD" and "OCPD" yet.

That restraint keeps the document descriptive.

A clinician may decide that Pattern B reflects anxiety, autism, trauma-related coping, another personality style, occupational conditioning, or ordinary traits. The point is to show that Pattern A does not explain everything.

The Treatment Meeting Question

If you already receive OCD treatment and suspect a second pattern, try:

Could we separate the behaviors that are maintained by obsessional fear and ritual relief from the broader standards or control patterns that do not seem to work that way?

Then ask:

If there are two mechanisms, how would that change the treatment plan?

You are not asking for a particular diagnosis. You are asking for the formulation to explain the data.

That is a reasonable clinical question.

Build Two Formulations Before One Conclusion

When you suspect comorbidity, resist the urge to create one blended label.

Write two separate formulations.

Pattern A: trigger, intrusive meaning, compulsion, short-term relief, cost.

Pattern B: standard, stance, control response, Reach, cost.

Then ask whether one formulation can explain the other without stretching.

If the only way to make everything "OCD" is to call every preferred rule a compulsion, the formulation may be too broad.

If the only way to make everything "OCPD" is to call unwanted intrusive thoughts another form of perfectionism, the formulation may also be too broad.

A clinician may still conclude that one diagnosis best explains both. The exercise simply prevents premature compression.

Comorbidity Changes the Treatment Conversation

When two processes are present, treatment planning may need two targets.

You can ask:

"Which behaviors are we treating as compulsions?"

"Which patterns are we treating as broad rigidity or perfectionism?"

"How will we know whether change in one area is affecting the other?"

This matters because improvement can be uneven.

A person may make major gains in contamination OCD and still struggle with delegation. Another may become more flexible about work standards while intrusive checking remains severe.

Uneven change is not automatically treatment failure. It may show that more than one mechanism needs attention.

Chapter 11: Why Treatment Fit Matters

A diagnosis matters partly because it changes what a treatment is trying to do.

This is the Treatment Fit lens.

It is also the chapter where overstatement is most dangerous.

ERP has strong evidence for OCD. OCPD has a smaller and less definitive treatment literature. That does **not** support the claim that ERP "does nothing" for every person with OCPD, nor does it support the claim that ERP is inherently harmful whenever OCPD is present. People can have both conditions, and clinicians may use exposure principles for specific fears or avoidance in a broader plan.

The defensible point is narrower: **a treatment should target the mechanism it is meant to change**.

What ERP Targets in OCD

ERP is a form of cognitive behavioral therapy used for OCD. In broad terms, exposure involves contacting feared thoughts, situations, sensations, or uncertainty, while response prevention involves reducing the compulsive behaviors or mental acts usually used to neutralize distress. NIMH identifies ERP as effective for reducing compulsive behaviors, and major clinical guidance supports CBT with ERP for OCD (National Institute of Mental Health, 2023; National Institute for Health and Care Excellence, 2005).

Suppose Ben repeatedly checks whether he harmed someone while driving.

An ERP formulation may identify triggers such as driving past pedestrians, obsessional doubt, urges to circle back, mirror checking, internet searches, or reassurance requests. Treatment is designed to help him face uncertainty without completing the ritualized attempts to obtain certainty.

That makes sense because the target is the obsession-compulsion cycle.

Now suppose Ben also controls how his team formats internal documents because he believes his method is the only professional standard. There may be no intrusive obsession, no feared catastrophe, and no ritualized relief cycle.

Calling that behavior an OCD compulsion simply because it is repetitive would be a formulation error.

What We Know About OCPD Treatment

Compared with OCD, the OCPD treatment evidence base is limited.

A 2022 clinical review described OCPD as common and impairing but emphasized that it has received relatively little research attention, particularly treatment research (Pinto et al., 2022). A 2022 systematic review of randomized medication trials found only a small evidence base and concluded that available findings were preliminary (Gecaite-Stonciene et al., 2022).

Clinical references discuss psychotherapy, including cognitive behavioral and psychodynamic approaches, while also noting sparse evidence (Zimmerman, 2026).

That asymmetry should make you skeptical of anyone who promises a single established OCPD protocol equivalent to ERP for OCD.

It should also make you skeptical of a book that confidently declares a treatment useless without evidence.

Mismatch Can Mean Several Things

If treatment does not seem to fit, there are many possible explanations.

The diagnosis may need review.

The diagnosis may be correct, but the formulation may be incomplete.

Two conditions may be present.

The treatment may be appropriate but poorly delivered, too brief, or not yet at an effective intensity.

The person may be doing covert rituals that make ERP look ineffective.

The target behavior may not be a compulsion.

A medical condition, substance, medication effect, neurodevelopmental difference, trauma history, mood disorder, or another psychological problem may need consideration.

The conclusion "ERP did not work, therefore I have OCPD" is not justified.

Treatment response is data. It is not a diagnostic test.

The Mechanism Interview

When treatment feels mismatched, ask the clinician to make the mechanism explicit.

Use these questions:

1. What is our formulation of the problem behavior?
2. What maintains it?
3. Which treatment component is intended to change that maintaining process?
4. What outcome would tell us the formulation is working?
5. If that outcome does not occur, when will we review the formulation?

These are ordinary questions about treatment logic.

A clinician may answer that your repeated checking is maintained by negative reinforcement through short-term anxiety reduction, so response prevention targets that cycle.

They may answer that rigid interpersonal rules are being addressed through work on cognitive flexibility, behavioral experiments, emotional awareness, interpersonal patterns, or another individualized approach.

The specific answer matters less than the presence of a coherent link.

Do Not Self-Administer a Diagnostic Switch

A common danger in health books is turning information into an instruction to abandon care.

Do not stop ERP, psychotherapy, or medication because a chapter made another diagnosis sound plausible. Do not add exposure exercises from a book to a complex clinical picture without considering whether they fit your plan.

If treatment feels wrong, bring evidence back to the clinician.

For example:

> *We have treated my repeated editing as a compulsion. I notice that I do not get an intrusive fear before it and I do not get anxiety relief after it. I believe the work should meet my standard and I become angry when asked to stop. Could we review whether this behavior belongs in the OCD formulation?*

That is a useful discrepancy.

Or:

> *I have been working on flexibility as though all my standards are personality-based, but I also have intrusive harm thoughts and repeated checking that gives short-term relief. Could we assess for an OCD loop?*

That is another.

When ERP "Feels Wrong"

ERP is supposed to be difficult. Feeling anxious during exposure does not mean the treatment is mismatched.

A better question is whether the exercise is targeting an obsessional trigger and reducing a compulsive or avoidant response.

If the answer is yes, discomfort may be part of appropriate treatment.

If the answer is unclear, ask.

If an exercise seems to target a broad value or ordinary preference as though it were a compulsion, ask how that target was selected.

If the therapist's explanation depends only on the fact that the behavior is repetitive or perfectionistic, ask for a more specific formulation.

Treatment quality includes understanding what is being treated.

Medication Is Not a Differential Test Either

Medication can be part of OCD care, commonly including serotonin reuptake inhibitors. NIMH notes that medication, psychotherapy, or a combination may be used depending on the person and severity (National Institute of Mental Health, 2023).

OCPD medication evidence is much thinner. The systematic review by Gecaite-Stonciene and colleagues found only limited randomized evidence and urged caution in interpreting it (Gecaite-Stonciene et al., 2022).

A response or nonresponse to medication does not prove one diagnosis.

The same medication can affect symptoms across conditions, and nonresponse can have many explanations.

Use medication history as one piece of clinical history, not as a home diagnostic experiment.

Build a Treatment Fit Sheet

If you are currently receiving care, fill this in with the actual treatment plan.

Question	Notes
Working diagnosis or formulation	
Main target behavior	
What starts the behavior	
What maintains it	
Treatment component	
Intended mechanism of change	
Outcome being tracked	
What has changed	
What has not changed	
Question for review	

This sheet can reveal a simple problem: sometimes the diagnosis is written down, but the treatment mechanism has never been explained.

You are allowed to ask for that explanation.

The next chapter looks more closely at what to do when ERP has felt irrelevant, confusing, or ineffective without using that experience as proof of a new label.

Ask for the Treatment Sentence

A treatment plan should be explainable in one sentence.

"We think repeated checking is maintained by short-term relief from obsessional doubt, so ERP is helping you face uncertainty without checking."

That sentence connects formulation and intervention.

A different sentence might be:

"We think your chronic overcontrol at work is maintained by rigid standards and difficulty tolerating alternative methods, so we are testing more flexible standards and examining the interpersonal consequences."

The exact wording will vary by clinician and approach.

If you cannot produce a sentence like this, ask for one.

Fit Is About Targets, Not Brand Names

Two therapists can both call their work CBT and target different mechanisms.

An exposure can be part of ERP for OCD, a behavioral experiment, a social-anxiety intervention, or another treatment plan.

A worksheet can be used to challenge obsessional beliefs, identify rigid standards, track mood, or organize behavior.

Do not judge fit by the label on the technique.

Ask what the technique is for in your case.

That question also keeps this book from becoming anti-ERP or pro-any-single-OCPD-treatment. The evidence does not justify either stance.

The useful position is more disciplined: identify the mechanism, choose a treatment with a rationale, measure the relevant outcome, and review when the data do not fit.

Chapter 12: When ERP Felt Wrong

A treatment can feel wrong for two very different reasons.

It can be correctly targeting the problem and asking you to do something genuinely difficult.

Or it can be working from a formulation that does not explain the behavior being targeted.

The feeling itself cannot tell you which one is happening.

This chapter gives you a way to examine the mismatch without turning treatment discomfort into a diagnosis.

First Separate Difficult From Irrelevant

ERP for OCD deliberately asks people to approach triggers and reduce rituals or avoidance. Anxiety, doubt, disgust, or incompleteness can rise during that work. Difficulty is therefore not evidence that ERP is inappropriate (National Institute of Mental Health, 2023).

An irrelevant exercise feels different.

Suppose Sofia checks the stove because of intrusive fire fears. Her clinician helps her leave the kitchen without photographing the knobs. The exercise directly targets a trigger and a compulsion. Sofia's anxiety rises. That is difficult, but the treatment logic is clear.

Now suppose a different clinician asks Rafael to submit a work document with uneven formatting because Rafael is "too perfectionistic." Rafael does not describe an intrusive fear or ritualized checking loop around formatting. His broader problem is that he believes there is one correct way for everyone to produce documents and repeatedly overrides other people's choices.

An exposure exercise could still conceivably be used in a broader behavioral plan, but calling the behavior an OCD compulsion without a clear obsession-compulsion formulation would require more explanation.

The question is not "Did I hate the exercise?"

The question is "What mechanism was the exercise designed to change?"

Common Reasons ERP Appears Not to Work

Treatment nonresponse is not a simple diagnostic signal.

A person may still be completing covert compulsions while avoiding visible ones. They may resist touching a doorknob but mentally reassure themselves for twenty minutes. They may stop asking a partner for reassurance and begin searching online instead.

The exposure may be too infrequent or disconnected from meaningful triggers.

The treatment may have become a reassurance exercise, with the therapist repeatedly explaining why the feared outcome is unlikely.

The person may have significant depression, trauma-related symptoms, substance use, neurodevelopmental needs, medical issues, or other conditions that complicate delivery.

The original formulation may be incomplete.

OCPD traits or another personality pattern may be shaping how the person approaches treatment.

These possibilities are reasons for review, not reasons to self-reassign a diagnosis.

Perfectionism Can Enter ERP Itself

A person can do ERP perfectionistically.

They build the perfect hierarchy. They rate every exposure with exact precision. They worry that a session "did not count" because anxiety was too low. They repeat an exercise until they are certain they did it correctly. They turn response prevention into a rule system.

Some of this can be OCD.

Some can reflect broader perfectionistic traits.

Some can be an understandable attempt to get control over a difficult treatment.

The clinical task is to determine what is happening.

If you find yourself trying to perform therapy perfectly, tell the therapist. That information can change how the work is framed.

Treatment Fit Versus Treatment Preference

A treatment can fit the mechanism and still not be your preferred experience.

You may dislike exposure and still have OCD.

You may prefer a more exploratory therapy and still need a clinician to explain what evidence supports the approach being recommended.

Preference matters because treatment requires participation. It does not by itself determine diagnosis.

Likewise, feeling understood by a particular diagnostic explanation does not prove it is correct. A formulation should account for observable patterns, history, impairment, and alternatives.

This protects you from a common internet loop: finding the label that produces the greatest feeling of recognition and treating recognition as validation.

Recognition can be the start of an assessment.

The Mismatch Inventory

If a treatment feels wrong, write one page before the next appointment.

Area	Observation
What behavior are we targeting?	
What happens immediately before it?	
What do I think or feel if I resist?	
What does doing it change immediately?	
What does my clinician think maintains it?	
What is the treatment supposed to change?	
What part feels mismatched?	
What evidence would make us review the formulation?	

Keep the final row open-ended.

You do not want the exercise to become "proof my therapist is wrong." You want it to make the disagreement precise.

How to Raise the Question Without Starting a Fight

A clinician can be wrong. A reader can be wrong. Both can have incomplete information.

Use language that focuses on discrepancies.

I want to understand the formulation better. We are treating this as a compulsion, but I cannot identify an intrusive fear or a relief cycle. I mostly experience it as a standard I believe is correct. What makes you see it as OCD?

Or:

We have focused on perfectionistic personality traits, but I have recurrent intrusive harm thoughts and repeated checking that temporarily reduces fear. Could we assess whether OCD is also present?

Or:

I know insight can vary. I do not want to use one feature as proof. Could we go through the pattern, duration, and function more systematically?

These questions invite reasoning.

When to Seek a Second Opinion

A second opinion can be reasonable when the diagnosis remains unclear, treatment repeatedly fails to match the described mechanism, important symptoms have not been assessed, or the clinician lacks experience with the relevant differential.

A second opinion is not automatically a rejection of the first clinician. It is another assessment.

If possible, look for someone with specific experience in OCD and ERP who also understands personality disorders, or a service able to assess both. Expertise matters because the overlap is easy to flatten.

Bring records rather than a prosecution brief.

Useful materials include a concise symptom timeline, examples of obsession-compulsion loops, examples of broad rigid standards, previous diagnoses, treatment history, medication history, and what changed or did not change.

Avoid sending fifty pages of internet research unless the clinician requests it. More material can make the central pattern harder to see.

If You Are Not in Treatment

You do not need to perform self-directed ERP in order to discover whether you have OCD.

You also do not need to prove OCPD by deliberately breaking all your routines.

The diagnostic question should come before ambitious self-treatment experiments when the picture is unclear.

Use the Five-Lens Difference Map to collect examples and look for a clinician who can assess them.

The strongest outcome from this book is not a home treatment plan. It is a better clinical question.

The Four Kinds of "Wrong"

When readers say ERP felt wrong, they may mean different things.

Too difficult: the exercise targeted a real obsession-compulsion loop, but distress was high.

Too confusing: the treatment rationale was never clear.

Too broad: ordinary preferences or broad personality patterns were labeled compulsions without a specific OCD formulation.

Too narrow: OCD work addressed rituals while another important problem remained untreated.

Name which kind you mean before drawing a conclusion.

"Too difficult" may call for better pacing or support within a sound plan.

"Too confusing" may call for a clearer explanation.

"Too broad" or "too narrow" may call for a formulation review.

Bring One Failed Exercise to Review

Choose one exercise that felt mismatched.

Write the trigger your therapist intended to target.

Write the compulsion or avoidance they intended you to reduce.

Write what actually happened.

Write what you believed the exercise was teaching.

Write what changed afterward.

This keeps the conversation specific.

"I hated ERP" can lead to an argument about treatment.

"In this exercise, we treated formatting as a compulsion, but I did not have an intrusive fear or relief cycle and I still believe the standard is correct" gives a clinician something to examine.

The reverse is also useful: "We treated this as perfectionism, but I was secretly performing mental reassurance the whole time."

Chapter 13: Build Your Evidence

A diagnostic appointment is a limited container.

You may have years of examples and forty-five minutes to explain them.

The solution is not to tell every story. It is to bring representative evidence.

This chapter turns the Five-Lens Difference Map into a one-page summary.

Start With Patterns, Not Labels

A weak opening sounds like this:

"I am sure I have OCPD instead of OCD because I read the criteria."

A stronger opening sounds like this:

"I was diagnosed with OCD two years ago. Some of my symptoms fit an obsession-compulsion pattern, but I also have longstanding rigidity and difficulty delegating that do not seem connected to intrusive fears. I would like help assessing whether one diagnosis explains both patterns."

The second statement gives the clinician a problem to solve.

It also leaves room for answers you did not expect.

Choose Representative Episodes

Do not choose the most dramatic episode just because it feels persuasive.

Choose examples that show the pattern clearly.

For possible OCD, a representative episode should help show:

the trigger;

the intrusive thought, image, urge, or sense of wrongness;

the compulsion, avoidance, reassurance, or mental response;

the short-term effect;

the time or functional cost.

For possible OCPD, a representative episode should help show:

the standard, rule, or control issue;

how strongly it was defended;

whether flexibility was possible;

whether the same pattern appears elsewhere;

the interpersonal or functional cost.

One clean example is more useful than fifteen vague claims.

Build a Timeline Without Rewriting Your Life

Clinicians may ask when patterns began and how they changed.

Memory is imperfect. Do not fabricate precision.

A simple timeline can use broad periods.

Period	OCD-like loops	Broad perfectionism/control patterns	Major context changes
Adolescence			
Early adulthood			
Last five years			
Current			

Context changes include major illness, trauma, pregnancy, caregiving, job changes, medication changes, substance use, sleep disruption, or other events that could affect symptoms.

The goal is not to explain causation. It is to prevent the assessment from treating every current behavior as though it has always existed.

Include What Does Not Fit

Readers often hide contradictory evidence because they are afraid it will weaken their case.

Contradictory evidence is exactly what differential diagnosis needs.

If you think OCPD fits but you also have unmistakably intrusive, unwanted obsessions and relief-producing rituals, include them.

If you think OCD fits but broad rules and interpersonal control have existed since early adulthood, include that too.

If you can be flexible at work but not at home, include that.

If the pattern appeared suddenly after a medical change, include that.

A good assessment is not a debate you win. It is a model that survives the inconvenient facts.

Measure Cost Concretely

"I am distressed" is important but broad.

Whenever possible, make cost observable.

"I spend about ninety minutes a night checking."

"I have missed three work deadlines this quarter because I kept refining completed tasks."

"My partner no longer shares certain household responsibilities because I redo them."

"I avoid driving alone because of hit-and-run fears."

"I have stopped inviting people over because I cannot tolerate how they move things."

Exact numbers are not required if you do not know them. Use conservative ranges rather than false precision.

Functioning gives a clinician something to compare over time.

Treatment History as Evidence

Previous treatment is part of the picture, but interpret it carefully.

Record:

Treatment	Target	Duration	What changed	What did not change
ERP				
Other psychotherapy				
Medication				
Self-help program				

Do not write "failed" when you mean "I completed four sessions." Do not write "worked" when you mean "I felt better for a week."

Describe the outcome.

This makes it easier to distinguish inadequate dose, poor fit, partial response, and a target that may have been misformulated.

The One-Page Differential Summary

Now assemble a page with six blocks.

1. Current question

One or two sentences explaining why you want the diagnosis or formulation reviewed.

2. Pattern A

A concise description of a possible obsession-compulsion loop.

3. Pattern B

A concise description of broad standards, perfectionism, control, or rigidity.

4. Reach and timeline

When the patterns began and where they appear.

5. Functional cost

Time, work, relationships, avoidance, distress, or other concrete effects.

6. Questions

Three questions you want the assessment to answer.

A completed example might read:

> ***Current question:*** *I have an OCD diagnosis, but not all of my difficulties seem connected to obsessions or compulsions. I want to understand whether OCPD traits, OCPD, both conditions, or another explanation should be considered.*

> ***Pattern A:*** *I get intrusive doubts that I hit someone while driving. I circle back, check mirrors, and search news reports. Checking lowers anxiety briefly. This happens several times a week.*

Pattern B: *Since my early twenties, I have had rigid work and household systems. I take tasks back from competent people if they use a different method. I usually believe my standard is correct, even when I see the conflict it creates.*

Reach and timeline: *Driving symptoms became severe three years ago. The control and delegation pattern has been present across work and home for more than a decade.*

Functional cost: *Driving avoidance, about five hours a week in checking, recurring conflict with my spouse, and two work deadlines missed after I redid delegated tasks.*

Questions: *Do these patterns belong to one diagnosis or more than one? What other explanations should we consider? How should the treatment plan distinguish the mechanisms?*

That page is not a self-diagnosis.

It is organized history.

Keep the Record From Becoming a Compulsion

If you have OCD, preparation itself can become compulsive.

You may rewrite the summary until every word feels safe. You may add evidence because you fear the clinician will misunderstand one detail. You may repeatedly compare it with diagnostic descriptions.

Set a practical limit.

One page. One revision. Three questions.

If you are working with an OCD clinician, you can tell them that preparing the document triggers a need for certainty. They may help you prevent the assessment process from becoming another ritual.

Ask for the Clinician's Model

At the end of an assessment, ask the professional to explain the formulation in plain language.

You can ask:

What pattern do you think best explains the symptoms I described?

Which features point away from the alternatives?

Is there anything important that remains uncertain?

How does the treatment plan follow from that formulation?

You are not asking for certainty that clinical work cannot provide. You are asking for reasoning.

That is a reasonable standard.

Choose Evidence That Discriminates

A good example does more than show severity.

It helps distinguish explanations.

"I spend four hours on work" shows cost.

"I spend four hours because every time I stop I get a new intrusive fear that an error will harm someone, and rechecking buys brief relief" adds mechanism.

"I spend four hours because I believe submitting work below my exact standard is irresponsible, and I reject my manager's lower standard" adds a different mechanism.

When space is limited, choose the example that shows the distinction.

Include a "What Would Change My Mind?" Line

At the bottom of your one-page summary, add:

What I would be open to hearing:

This can be simple.

"That my broad rigidity is better explained by another condition."

"That both patterns are part of OCD."

"That I have OCPD traits but do not meet criteria for the disorder."

"That more history is needed."

The line is not a test of open-mindedness. It reminds you that the appointment is an assessment rather than a confirmation session.

If you notice yourself trying to make the page impossible to disagree with, stop editing. That urge is more useful to report than another paragraph of evidence.

Chapter 14: Reopen the Diagnostic Question

A diagnosis can feel permanent because it enters a chart.

It is not a tattoo.

Clinical formulations can be revisited when new information appears, symptoms change, treatment response raises questions, or a broader history becomes visible.

Reopening the question does not require accusing anyone of negligence.

It requires a clear reason.

Decide What You Are Asking For

"I want to know if my diagnosis is wrong" is understandable but broad.

There are several more specific requests:

review the existing OCD diagnosis;

assess for OCPD or clinically significant OCPD traits;

assess whether both conditions are present;

review other differential possibilities;

review whether current treatment targets the right mechanism.

You may need more than one.

Write the request in one sentence before the appointment.

Example:

I would like a differential review of my OCD diagnosis because some difficulties fit an obsession-compulsion loop and others are longstanding patterns of perfectionism, control, and delegation that do not seem connected to obsessions.

That sentence gives the appointment a task.

Lead With the Mismatch

If you begin with diagnostic vocabulary, a clinician may hear a conclusion.

If you begin with a mismatch, they hear a clinical problem.

For example:

My harm checking responds to ERP, but the broader conflict about standards and control has not changed and does not feel driven by intrusive fears.

Or:

I was told my rigidity was OCPD, but I have recurrent unwanted thoughts and mental rituals that were never assessed.

Or:

I was diagnosed after a short appointment, and I do not remember being asked about the function, duration, or breadth of these behaviors.

A mismatch is harder to dismiss because it points to data.

Ask About Differential Diagnosis Directly

You do not have to speak in hints.

Try:

How did you distinguish OCD from OCPD in my case?

What evidence supports OCD for this specific behavior?

What evidence would make you consider OCPD or another explanation?

Could both conditions be present?

How does my level of insight affect your reasoning?

Which parts of my history do not fit your current formulation?

These questions are collaborative when asked in good faith.

They also reveal whether the diagnosis has been considered at the level of mechanism or only at the level of familiar labels.

When a Clinician Says "You Cannot Have Both"

That statement should prompt clarification.

OCD and OCPD are distinct diagnoses that can co-occur, and clinical literature specifically addresses comorbid presentations (Wheaton et al., 2022).

You can say:

I understood that the two conditions can co-occur. Are you saying you do not think both are present in my case, or that they cannot occur together?

The distinction matters.

A clinician may have meant that your particular symptoms are better explained by one condition. That is a clinical judgment.

A categorical claim that the diagnoses are mutually exclusive would require correction.

When a Clinician Dismisses OCPD as "Just Perfectionism"

OCPD is not synonymous with being perfectionistic.

It involves a broader and clinically significant pattern of order, perfectionism, and control with rigidity and functional or relational consequences (Pinto et al., 2022).

You might respond:

> *I agree that perfectionism alone is not enough. I am concerned about a broader pattern across delegation, work, finances, and relationships. Could we review whether that pattern is clinically significant?*

Again, bring examples.

The goal is not to force a diagnosis. It is to make sure the relevant pattern is actually assessed.

When a Clinician Dismisses OCD Because You Defend Some Behaviors

Remember the insight chapter.

You may defend some standards and still have separate intrusive obsessions and compulsions. OCD can also occur with varying insight.

Say:

> *Some of my standards feel reasonable to me, but I also have a separate pattern of intrusive thoughts I do not want and rituals that temporarily reduce distress. Could we assess those separately?*

Separating behaviors is often more productive than arguing over which single label describes your whole personality.

If the Clinician Disagrees

A thoughtful disagreement is different from dismissal.

A clinician may review your examples and conclude that OCPD is unlikely. They may identify another condition. They may believe that the broad rigidity is better explained by autism, anxiety, trauma, depression, culture, occupational conditioning, or nonclinical personality traits. They may need more history.

Ask for the reasoning.

Which observations make OCPD less likely?

What alternative explains the broad pattern better?

What would we expect to see if your formulation is correct?

You can then decide whether the explanation makes sense, whether to continue the work, or whether another qualified opinion would be useful.

Bring a Partner Carefully

A partner can add information about Reach, accommodation, conflict, and change over time, if you want them involved and the clinician agrees.

Set the purpose before the session.

The purpose is not for the partner to prove that you are controlling.

It is to provide observations.

A useful partner statement might be:

I notice that after intrusive fears, she asks me the same reassurance question until anxiety comes down. Separately, there are longstanding rules about how I complete ordinary tasks, and disagreement about those rules creates conflict. I would like help understanding whether those are the same process.

That gives the clinician two sequences to examine.

Document the Outcome

After the appointment, write down four things:

1. What the clinician thinks the main formulation is.
2. What remains uncertain.
3. What treatment target follows from the formulation.

4. What would trigger another review.

Do not turn the notes into a transcript.

You are creating a decision record.

If the answer is "We need more information," that can be a legitimate outcome. Differential diagnosis sometimes improves through observation over time rather than one decisive appointment.

The Reassessment Script

Here is a concise script you can adapt:

I want to revisit the formulation, not because I need a particular diagnosis but because I see two patterns. One involves intrusive, unwanted thoughts and repetitive responses that give short-term relief. The other is a longstanding pattern of standards, perfectionism, and control that I often believe is justified, even though it creates problems. I would like us to assess whether OCD explains both, whether OCPD traits or OCPD should be considered, whether both may be present, and what other explanations we should keep open. I also want to understand how the answer changes the treatment targets.

That is the question this book was built to help you ask.

A Review Can End With the Same Diagnosis

Reassessment does not have to produce a new label to be worthwhile.

A clinician may review the evidence and explain why the original OCD diagnosis still accounts for the behavior you questioned. They may identify obsessional responsibility or incompleteness that was previously hidden.

They may conclude that OCPD traits are present but not pervasive or impairing enough for the diagnosis.

They may find that another condition explains the rigidity better.

A useful review improves the formulation even when the diagnostic code stays the same.

Ask What Would Be Documented Differently

If the clinician sees more than one process, ask how that difference will appear in the treatment plan.

Will different target behaviors be tracked?

Will partner accommodation be addressed separately from interpersonal control?

Will a personality assessment be scheduled?

Will ERP continue for specific OCD loops while other therapy work addresses broader rigidity?

Will another specialist be consulted?

This converts diagnostic language into practical care.

The question "What changes because we learned this?" is often more useful than arguing about the label itself.

Chapter 15: Thirty Days of Better Questions

The end of a differential guide should not be a quiz result.

It should be a better record.

The next thirty days are designed to help you gather enough representative information to improve a clinical conversation without making observation itself into a full-time project.

There are four weeks and one final preparation step.

If you are currently in treatment, share the plan with your clinician if that would help keep the work aligned with therapy.

Week 1: Observe the Sequence

For seven days, record no more than one episode per day.

Choose episodes that actually cost time, create distress, or cause conflict. Do not record every preference.

Use three lines:

Trigger: What happened first?

Response: What did you do?

Immediate effect: What changed in the next few minutes?

That is all.

Do not diagnose the episode.

The purpose of Week 1 is to break the habit of naming behavior without seeing the sequence.

At the end of the week, review the entries once. Look for repeated immediate effects.

Does checking repeatedly reduce fear?

Does correction restore a preferred sense of order?

Does reassurance reduce doubt?

Does taking work back from someone else restore control?

If nothing repeats, keep the uncertainty.

Week 2: Add Stance

For Week 2, add one question:

What was my relationship to the thought, rule, urge, or standard?

Use plain words.

"Unwanted."

"Felt true."

"Felt morally necessary."

"Felt like my rule."

"Felt frightening to ignore."

"Felt irritating when others disagreed."

"Not sure."

Avoid trying to decide whether the entry is ego-dystonic or ego-syntonic. Those terms are useful after you have described the experience.

At the end of Week 2, compare stance with function.

A thought can feel true and still participate in an OCD loop.

A rule can feel costly and still be defended as correct.

The paired information matters.

Week 3: Map Reach

Now stop focusing only on episodes and look across settings.

Use this grid.

Domain	Possible obsession-compulsion loops	Possible standards/control patterns	Cost
Work or school			
Home			
Close relationships			
Money and possessions			

Domain	Possible obsession-compulsion loops	Possible standards/control patterns	Cost
Travel and plans			
Health and safety			
Morality or responsibility			

The goal is to see breadth.

A specific OCD theme may be intense but relatively bounded.

An OCPD pattern is expected to be pervasive rather than confined to a single obsessional topic.

Real cases are messier. OCD can have many themes. OCPD traits can be stronger in some domains than others.

Use the grid as a map, not a rule.

Week 4: Review Treatment Fit

If you are in treatment, complete the Treatment Fit sheet from Chapter 11.

If you are not, write down any past treatments and what they appeared to target.

Then ask:

Which behaviors have been treated as compulsions?

What evidence supports that formulation?

Which broad patterns have not changed even when OCD symptoms improved?

Which intrusive loops have not been explained by a personality formulation?

What do I want a clinician to assess next?

This is the week when the first three lenses become a clinical question.

Day 29: Build the One-Page Summary

Use the structure from Chapter 13.

Keep it to one page.

If you feel compelled to make it exhaustive, that is a useful moment to practice stopping. A summary is supposed to leave information out.

Include:

the current question;

one representative possible OCD loop;

one representative broad rigidity/perfectionism pattern, if present;

timeline and reach;

concrete costs;

treatment history in one or two lines;

three questions for the clinician.

Do not add a self-assigned diagnosis at the top.

Day 30: Prepare the Conversation

Read the one-page summary once.

Then write your opening sentence.

Examples:

I want to understand whether all of my symptoms are being explained by the right mechanism.

I have an OCD diagnosis, but some longstanding control and perfectionism patterns do not fit the obsession-compulsion loop as I understand it.

I have been described as having OCPD traits, but I also have intrusive thoughts and rituals that I want assessed for OCD.

I wonder whether both processes could be present.

Choose one.

The appointment does not need a speech.

A Thirty-Day Tracker

Day	Focus	Done
1 to 7	One Trigger, Response, Immediate Effect entry per day	

Day	Focus	Done
8 to 14	Add Stance to one entry per day	
15 to 21	Review Reach across settings	
22 to 28	Review Treatment Fit and history	
29	Create one-page summary	
30	Prepare three questions and opening sentence	

The empty column is not a score.

Missed days do not need to be made up.

This is an information-gathering plan, not a compliance test.

What Not to Do for Thirty Days

Do not repeatedly search diagnostic criteria to see whether your latest episode "counts."

Do not ask friends to vote on which diagnosis you have.

Do not use a partner as a reassurance source for every entry.

Do not deliberately provoke severe symptoms to collect better examples.

Do not stop prescribed treatment in order to see which pattern appears.

Better evidence comes from ordinary life.

The Final Five-Lens Review

At the end of thirty days, choose two patterns and complete the map.

Lens	Pattern 1	Pattern 2
Trigger		
Stance		
Function		
Reach		
Treatment Fit		

Now ask only three interpretive questions:

1. Does one formulation clearly fail to explain an important part of the picture?
2. Is there evidence that two different maintaining processes may be present?
3. What does a qualified clinician need to assess next?

These are better questions than "Which box am I?"

If the Answer Still Feels Unclear

Unclear is a legitimate ending.

The conditions share features. Insight varies. Comorbidity is possible. Perfectionism is not specific to either disorder. Other diagnoses and life contexts can mimic parts of the picture.

The purpose of a differential guide is not to guarantee that uncertainty disappears.

It is to make uncertainty more specific.

"I do not know what is wrong with me" is a frighteningly large question.

"I have intrusive harm doubts followed by checking and short-term relief, plus a separate longstanding pattern of rigid standards and delegation problems; I want both assessed" is a smaller, more workable question.

That difference is the practical result of the book.

Keep the Project Smaller Than Your Life

Thirty days is a container.

It should not turn every meal, email, argument, and thought into data.

Choose ordinary examples and then return to living.

A useful rule is one entry, one review, one next step.

One entry records the episode.

One review at the end of the week looks for a pattern.

One next step becomes a question for care.

If you notice that you are recording because you fear forgetting evidence, set a smaller limit. If you notice that you are collecting examples to prove another person wrong, return to your own observations.

Decide What Happens on Day 31

The journal needs an exit.

Write one of these:

"I will bring the summary to my current clinician."

"I will look for an assessment with someone experienced in OCD and personality disorders."

"I will discuss the question with my primary care clinician and ask about referral."

"I will pause diagnostic research until my next appointment."

"I will keep the current formulation unless new evidence appears."

A project without an exit can become endless self-monitoring.

The aim of thirty days is not to become an expert in your own differential diagnosis. It is to bring better information to the person whose role is to assess it.

Conclusion: Clarity Before Certainty

OCD and OCPD are easy to confuse when you begin with appearance.

Both can involve repetition. Both can involve checking. Both can involve perfectionism, rules, doubt, and difficulty letting go. Both can create conflict. Both can consume time.

The difference becomes clearer when you ask what the behavior is doing.

The Five-Lens Difference Map has given you five questions:

Trigger: What starts the pattern?

Stance: How do you relate to the thought, rule, urge, or standard?

Function: What is the behavior trying to accomplish right now?

Reach: Is this a symptom loop, or a broad pattern across settings and years?

Treatment Fit: What mechanism is the intervention trying to change?

None of those questions is diagnostic on its own.

Together, they help prevent several common mistakes.

They prevent you from calling every neat habit OCD.

They prevent you from calling every unwanted perfectionistic behavior OCPD.

They prevent you from using ego-dystonic and ego-syntonic as a binary test.

They make room for both conditions to be present.

They make treatment response one piece of evidence rather than a home diagnostic procedure.

Most importantly, they give you language that can travel from private confusion into a clinical room.

You do not need to arrive with the answer.

You need to arrive with a pattern that can be assessed.

If one behavior is driven by an intrusive fear and a ritual that buys a few minutes of relief, say that.

If another behavior is part of a longstanding system of standards and control that you often believe is correct, say that.

If your partner sees a broader reach than you do, consider bringing that observation with consent and without turning it into a verdict.

If ERP has helped one symptom and left another untouched, ask whether there are two targets.

If ERP feels difficult, do not assume difficulty means mismatch. Ask what mechanism the exercise is meant to change.

If a diagnosis does not explain the data, it is reasonable to ask for the formulation to be revisited.

The goal is not certainty at any cost.

OCD itself can make certainty an especially dangerous prize. OCPD-related rigidity can make the "right" conceptual answer feel as though it must be defended. A differential process that becomes another demand for a perfect conclusion has missed its purpose.

A better endpoint is flexible clarity.

You know what you have observed. You know where the observations point. You know which parts remain ambiguous. You know what questions to take to someone qualified to examine them.

That is enough to move the diagnostic conversation forward.

Appendix A: Five-Lens Difference Map Worksheets

This appendix collects the book's observation tools in one place.

These worksheets are not diagnostic instruments. They do not have validated cutoffs, and they should not be scored. Their purpose is to help you describe patterns clearly enough for a clinician to assess.

If you have OCD and notice that completing or reviewing a worksheet is becoming a reassurance ritual, reduce the task. One representative entry is enough.

Worksheet 1: One Behavior, Five Lenses

Behavior: Describe one action in concrete terms.

Avoid: "I am controlling."

Prefer: "I reopen completed invoices three or four times after sending them."

Lens	Prompt	Notes
Trigger	What happened immediately before the urge or behavior?	
Stance	Did the thought or standard feel unwanted, doubtful, necessary, correct, frightening, irritating, or something else?	
Function	What changed immediately after you acted?	
Reach	Where else does this pattern appear, and for how long?	
Treatment Fit	If this has been treated, what mechanism was the intervention designed to change?	

Cost: What did the episode cost in time, energy, opportunity, or relationship strain?

Uncertainty: What part of the sequence do you not understand yet?

Worksheet 2: Possible OCD Loop

Use this only to describe a sequence that appears to involve intrusive thoughts, urges, images, uncertainty, incompleteness, or another obsessional trigger.

Step	Prompt	Notes
Trigger	Situation, thought, image, sensation, or uncertainty	
Obsessional meaning	What did you fear the experience meant or could cause?	
Response	Checking, washing, avoidance, reassurance, reviewing, neutralizing, or another act	
Immediate effect	Did anxiety, guilt, disgust, doubt, or incompleteness change?	
Return	How and when did the doubt or urge return?	
Cost	Time, distress, avoidance, conflict, or lost opportunity	

Important: If you cannot identify an obsessional process, write "unclear." Do not invent a feared consequence to make the form fit.

Worksheet 3: Possible Broad Standards and Control Pattern

Use this to describe a longstanding rule, perfectionistic standard, or control issue.

Prompt	Notes
What is the rule or standard?	
Why does it feel important or correct?	
What happens when another competent person uses a different method?	
What happens when a deadline requires "good enough"?	

Prompt	Notes
Can the rule change when circumstances change?	
Where else does a similar pattern appear?	
How long has it been present?	
What does it cost you?	
What does it cost other people?	

Counterfactual: If there were no anxiety attached to the situation, would you still want the rule followed?

Worksheet 4: Stance Without Jargon

Choose one thought, rule, urge, or standard.

Question	Answer
Did it arrive against my wishes?	
Do I believe it is true?	
Do I believe it is morally or practically correct?	
Do I want to keep it?	
Do I dislike the pattern, the consequences, or both?	
What happens if I do not act on it?	
How certain am I about the belief in the moment?	
How certain am I later?	

This separates several experiences that are often compressed into the words ego-dystonic and ego-syntonic.

Worksheet 5: Reach Across Life

Domain	Repetitive fear/doubt loop?	Standards/control pattern?	Since when?	Cost

Domain	Repetitive fear/doubt loop?	Standards/control pattern?	Since when?	Cost
Work or school				
Home				
Close relationships				
Money				
Possessions				
Health and safety				
Travel and plans				
Morality or responsibility				
Leisure and rest				

A broad pattern does not automatically mean OCPD. A narrow pattern does not automatically mean OCD. Reach is one lens.

Worksheet 6: Treatment Fit

Question	Notes
What diagnosis or formulation is treatment based on?	
What exact behavior is being targeted?	
What is believed to trigger it?	
What is believed to maintain it?	
What treatment component addresses that process?	
What outcome is being measured?	
What improved?	
What did not improve?	
What feels difficult but relevant?	
What feels irrelevant to the described mechanism?	

Question	Notes
What question should be reviewed with the clinician?	

Do not use this sheet to decide independently whether treatment should stop.

Worksheet 7: Partner Observation

Complete only if both people agree to use it constructively.

Prompt	Partner's observation
What usually happens immediately before the problem?	
What does the person ask me to do?	
If I comply, what happens next?	
Does relief last, or does the question return?	
Is the request about certainty/safety or about doing things a particular way?	
Where else does this pattern appear?	
What is the impact on me or the household?	
What am I unsure about?	

Do not write a diagnosis in the final row.

Worksheet 8: Work Pattern

Pattern	Example	Frequency/time	Function	Cost
Rechecking				
Rewriting				
Redoing others' work				
Difficulty delegating				
Avoiding responsibility				

Pattern	Example	Frequency/time	Function	Cost
Overpreparing				
Conflict over methods				
Reassurance/ approval seeking				

Then ask: does the same structure appear outside work?

Worksheet 9: Perfectionism Autopsy

Choose a task that took materially longer than expected.

Actual requirement:

Point when requirement was met:

Work continued after that point:

What made stopping difficult:

What I feared or believed would happen if I stopped:

Whether another competent person's work at the same quality would have been acceptable:

Short-term effect of continuing:

Cost of continuing:

Question for a clinician:

Worksheet 10: One-Page Differential Summary

Keep the completed version to one page.

Current question

Why are you asking for a review?

Pattern A

Describe one possible obsession-compulsion loop.

Pattern B

Describe one possible broad standards/control pattern.

Reach and timeline

When did each begin, and where does each appear?

Functional cost

Time, distress, avoidance, work effects, relationship effects, or other concrete consequences.

Treatment history

What has been tried, what was targeted, and what changed?

Three questions

1.

2.

3.

Stop after three.

Appendix B: Conversation Scripts

Scripts are scaffolding. They are not magic sentences.

Use the wording that sounds natural in your voice. The important feature is the structure: observation first, question second, conclusion left open.

Asking for a Diagnostic Review

I would like to revisit the formulation because not all of my symptoms seem to work the same way. Some involve intrusive thoughts followed by repetitive responses that give short-term relief. Others involve longstanding rules and control patterns that I often believe are justified. Could we assess whether one diagnosis explains both, whether more than one condition may be present, and what other explanations we should consider?

Asking How OCD Was Distinguished From OCPD

Could you explain which features in my history led you toward OCD rather than OCPD for this behavior? I am trying to understand the mechanism, not just the label.

Asking How OCPD Was Distinguished From OCD

I understand why the broad perfectionism and control pattern raised OCPD. I also have intrusive thoughts and repetitive checking that lowers anxiety for a short time. How are you accounting for that part of the picture?

Asking About Both Conditions

I know the diagnoses are distinct, but I understand they can co-occur. Do you think one condition explains my presentation, or should we assess whether both processes are present?

Asking About Insight

Some of my rules feel correct to me and some of my thoughts feel intrusive and unwanted. I also know insight in OCD can vary. How much weight are you giving my stance toward each behavior?

Asking About Treatment Mechanism

What do you think maintains this behavior, and which part of treatment is intended to change that process?

Asking Why an Exercise Is ERP

I want to understand the target. What is the obsessional trigger in this exercise, what response are we preventing, and how does the exercise connect to my formulation?

Raising a Mismatch

The checking we have targeted does not seem to give me anxiety relief, and I cannot identify an intrusive fear before it. I mostly experience it as a standard I believe is correct. Could we review whether we are describing the function accurately?

Raising a Possible Hidden Compulsion

We have been working on broad perfectionism, but I notice that I spend a lot of time mentally reviewing after intrusive thoughts. The reviewing reduces distress briefly. Could that be a compulsion that needs separate assessment?

Asking for a Second Opinion Referral

I appreciate the work we have done. The differential still feels unclear, and I would like another assessment from someone with experience in both OCD and personality disorders. Can you help me identify an appropriate referral?

Partner: Describing Reassurance

I notice that after a fear appears, I am asked the same question several times. My answers seem to help for a few minutes and then the doubt returns. I would like guidance on how to respond without making the cycle stronger.

Partner: Describing Control

I notice that many ordinary household tasks have one accepted method, and when I use a different competent method the task is often corrected or redone. I am not trying to assign a diagnosis. I want the impact and the breadth of that pattern included in the assessment.

Partner: Setting a Reassurance Boundary

If a clinician has helped you make a plan:

I know you are distressed. I am going to follow the reassurance plan we agreed rather than answer the question again.

Without a treatment plan, avoid pretending the script is therapy. You can say:

I can see that this question is not settling even after repeated answers. I think we need help deciding how to respond to the pattern.

Partner: Setting a Method Boundary

I am willing to be responsible for this task. If I am responsible for it, I need room to complete it competently in my own way. If there is a real safety or outcome requirement, let us agree on that requirement rather than one person's preferred method.

Work: Asking for a Clear Standard

What is the actual acceptance standard for this task, and what would count as unnecessary refinement beyond that standard?

This is useful when you suspect the internal standard has drifted beyond the real requirement.

Work: Delegation

I want to separate outcome requirements from method preferences. Which parts of the process are mandatory, and which can the person doing the task decide?

When You Are Unsure

I do not know whether this is OCD, OCPD, both, or something else. What I can describe is the sequence and the cost. Can we start there?

That last script may be the most useful one in the appendix.

Appendix C: Clinician Visit Pack

This section is designed to be printed or copied into a note.

It helps you enter an appointment with concise information rather than a pile of disconnected examples.

Page 1: Reason for Review

My current diagnosis or working formulation:

Who made it and approximately when:

What treatment has been based on it:

Why I am asking for review now:

Complete the final line with a discrepancy.

Examples:

"ERP reduced contamination rituals but did not change a longstanding pattern of rigid standards and difficulty delegating."

"I have been treated for perfectionism, but intrusive harm thoughts and repeated checking have not been assessed as possible OCD."

"I recognize both an obsession-compulsion loop and a broad control pattern."

Avoid:

"I know my clinician was wrong."

The visit should begin with data.

Page 2: Pattern A

Concrete behavior:

Trigger:

Thought, image, urge, rule, or standard:

Stance toward it:

Response:

Immediate effect:

How long the effect lasts:

Where else it appears:

How long the pattern has existed:

Functional cost:

Page 3: Pattern B

Repeat the same fields for a second pattern that seems to work differently.

Do not choose two examples that are nearly identical. The purpose is to show the differential problem.

Page 4: Timeline

Use broad dates if exact dates are uncertain.

Before age 18, if relevant and remembered:

Early adulthood:

Later adulthood:

Major changes in severity:

Major life or medical context around changes:

Previous periods of remission or reduced symptoms:

A clinician may ask developmental questions because personality-disorder assessment requires attention to enduring patterns, while OCD can also begin early and change in severity over time.

Page 5: Treatment History

For each treatment, write only what you know.

Therapy type:

Approximate duration:

Main target:

What I actually did in treatment:

What improved:

What did not improve:

Why it ended:

Medication, if relevant:

Dose and duration, if known:

Benefit or side effects:

Do not guess doses or dates.

Page 6: Functional Cost

Mark only areas with a meaningful effect.

Time: How much time do patterns take?

Work or school: Deadlines, avoidance, overwork, conflict, reduced output.

Relationships: Reassurance, correction, arguments, withdrawal, role changes.

Home: Routines, chores, control, avoidance.

Money: Spending, saving, checking, decision paralysis.

Health: Sleep, stress, missed care, compulsive health behavior.

Leisure: Activities lost to work, rituals, avoidance, or inflexibility.

Safety: Any urgent concern that requires immediate attention.

Page 7: Questions for the Clinician

Choose three to five.

1. What formulation best explains Pattern A?
2. What formulation best explains Pattern B?
3. What makes OCD more or less likely?
4. What makes OCPD more or less likely?
5. Could both conditions be present?
6. What other explanations should be assessed?
7. How does insight affect the differential in my case?
8. What treatment mechanism follows from your formulation?
9. How will we know whether the treatment is targeting the right process?
10. When should we review the formulation again?

What to Leave Out

Leave out copied diagnostic criteria unless the clinician asks for them.

Leave out screenshots from dozens of social-media posts.

Leave out a long argument for why one label must be correct.

Leave out a score from an unvalidated online quiz.

Bring the shortest document that makes the pattern visible.

Appendix D: Quick Comparison Reference

This reference condenses distinctions discussed throughout the book. It is not a diagnostic chart.

Topic	OCD	OCPD	Important caution
Diagnostic family	Obsessive-compulsive and related disorder	Personality disorder	Different diagnostic categories can still co-occur
Core clinical pattern	Obsessions, compulsions, or both	Pervasive order, perfectionism, and control	Neither should be inferred from neatness alone
Trigger	Often intrusive thought, image, urge, uncertainty, disgust, or incompleteness	Often rule violation, different method, imperfection, loss of control, or productivity concern	Triggers vary widely
Stance	Often unwanted or distressing	Often experienced as justified or consistent with standards	Insight and ambivalence vary
Function	Ritual may reduce distress or seek certainty	Behavior may enforce standards or restore control	Same behavior can have mixed functions
Reach	Can center on specific themes, though themes can multiply	Expected to be broad and enduring	Reach is not a single-test rule
Checking	Can be a compulsion	Can be quality/control behavior	Context and function are essential
Perfectionism	Can serve certainty or "just right" compulsions	Can interfere with completion and flexibility	Perfectionism occurs outside both diagnoses
Delegation	May be affected by responsibility fears or avoidance	Difficulty delegating unless others conform can be prominent	Workplace structure matters
Relationships	Reassurance and accommodation may dominate	Correction, standards, and control may dominate	Both can strain relationships

Topic	OCD	OCPD	Important caution
Insight	Can range from good to absent/delusional beliefs under DSM specifiers	Standards often feel defensible, but consequences can be distressing	Ego-dystonic/ego-syntonic is a clue, not a verdict
ERP	Strong evidence as OCD treatment	Not an established OCPD-specific treatment protocol	A person with both may still receive ERP for OCD
Medication	SSRIs and other options can be used in OCD care	Evidence for medication is limited	Medication response does not diagnose
Comorbidity	OCPD can co-occur	OCD can co-occur	"Versus" does not mean mutually exclusive
Assessment	Symptoms, impairment, history, insight, differentials	Pervasive pattern, history, impairment, differentials	Qualified clinical assessment is required

Ten Reminders

1. Neatness is not OCD.
2. Perfectionism is not OCPD by itself.
3. An unwanted thought is not automatically an obsession in the diagnostic sense.
4. A repeated act is not automatically a compulsion.
5. A defended rule is not automatically OCPD.
6. Insight varies.
7. Function matters more than appearance.
8. Reach matters.
9. Both conditions can occur together.
10. Treatment response is data, not a home diagnostic test.

Appendix E: Side-by-Side Casebook

The cases in this appendix are composites. They are designed to show how the Five-Lens Difference Map changes the question. They are not portraits of specific people and should not be used as templates for self-diagnosis.

Case 1: The Sent Email

Nadia

Nadia sends a routine email to her manager. Ten minutes later she has a sudden thought that one sentence could be read as insulting. She reopens the sent message. The sentence looks fine, but she imagines another interpretation. She asks a friend to read it. Relief lasts until she wonders whether the friend was only being kind.

Trigger: intrusive doubt after sending.

Stance: she does not want the thought and wishes she could leave the message alone.

Function: rereading and reassurance lower anxiety temporarily.

Reach: similar loops occur around morality and relationships, but she is not broadly rigid about how other people work.

Treatment Fit question: could this be an OCD reassurance and checking loop?

Rafael

Rafael sends a project email. He reopens it because the bullets are not parallel and the subject line is less precise than he prefers. He edits future drafts for the team and creates a template everyone is expected to use. When a colleague says clients do not care about the formatting, Rafael says that professional work should not depend on whether a client notices.

Trigger: work falls short of his preferred standard.

Stance: the standard feels correct.

Function: revision restores a sense that the work meets the standard.

Reach: similar standards govern reports, calendars, household organization, and travel planning.

Treatment Fit question: is the broad pattern of perfectionism and control clinically significant, and what else should be assessed?

What the photograph misses

Both people reread email.

The sequence underneath is different.

Case 2: The Locked Door

Ben

Ben locks the front door, walks to the car, and gets an image of someone entering the house. He remembers turning the key but does not trust the memory. He checks again. On the second walk to the car, he wonders whether he pulled the handle hard enough. The checking repeats.

Trigger: intrusive image and doubt.

Stance: unwanted and distressing.

Function: checking reduces fear and responsibility for a short time.

Reach: strongest around safety themes.

Treatment Fit question: does the pattern fit OCD checking, and how should ERP address it?

Elena

Elena has a household departure routine: windows checked, thermostat set, lights off, doors checked in a fixed order. She becomes annoyed when family members skip steps. She does not describe a recurring intrusive image or temporary relief cycle. She argues that a well-run household should have procedures and that other people are careless.

Trigger: deviation from procedure.

Stance: rule feels justified.

Function: completing the routine restores order and confidence in the system.

Reach: detailed procedures also govern chores, packing, bills, and meal planning.

Treatment Fit question: what is the broader pattern, and does it meet criteria for a personality disorder or another explanation?

What the photograph misses

Both people check a door.

The count of checks tells less than the function.

Case 3: The Child's Lunch

Sofia

Sofia prepares her child's lunch and suddenly fears that a trace of cleaning chemical could be on the container. She washes it again. Then she worries that the sponge itself was contaminated. She changes the sponge, rewashes the container, and eventually throws the food away.

She knows the sequence is becoming unreasonable, but the possibility of causing harm feels impossible to accept.

Possible OCD markers to assess: intrusive contamination fear, responsibility, repeated neutralizing, temporary relief, escalating rules.

Marcus

Marcus prepares lunches according to a detailed nutrition plan. He weighs portions and becomes upset when his partner substitutes a different but nutritionally reasonable food. He says consistency matters and accuses his partner of being undisciplined. The same standard-centered conflicts appear around exercise, spending, and scheduling.

Possible OCPD markers to assess: broad standards, inflexibility, control of others' methods, cost to relationships.

A third possibility

Priya has a child with a medically documented severe food allergy and follows a detailed contamination protocol recommended by the medical team.

The behavior is careful because the risk is real.

Context prevents the comparison from pathologizing appropriate safety.

Case 4: The Missed Deadline

Lucas

Lucas misses a deadline because he repeatedly checks every statistic against the original database. He fears that a single wrong number could lead senior staff to make a harmful decision. Each completed check produces a new doubt about whether he checked the right version.

The organization already has a validated quality-control process, and his extra checking is not required.

Possible OCD process: responsibility obsession followed by checking that does not produce lasting certainty.

Theo

Theo misses a deadline because he keeps refining the structure, style, and completeness of a document. His manager says the work met the requirement two days earlier. Theo disagrees. He sees the deadline as less important than submitting work he considers fully correct.

He uses the same standard on low-stakes and high-stakes tasks.

Possible OCPD process: perfectionism that interferes with completion and difficulty adjusting standards to context.

Another possibility

Daniel misses the deadline because he has untreated ADHD and repeatedly underestimates task-switching costs.

The symptom "missed deadline" is not specific.

Case 5: The Reassurance Argument

Aisha

Aisha asks her partner whether a skin mark looks dangerous. Her partner says no. Aisha asks whether he looked closely. He takes a photograph and zooms in. She feels calmer for ten minutes, then thinks the color may have changed.

The couple has spent much of the evening trying to settle the same question.

Function: reassurance and checking reduce health anxiety temporarily.

A clinician would still need to distinguish OCD, illness anxiety, and other possibilities.

Jordan

Jordan asks his partner to confirm that the monthly budget was followed. When the partner says yes, Jordan reviews the spending and finds a small unplanned purchase. He launches into a long explanation about financial discipline and insists they use his category system next month.

Jordan is not seeking certainty that fades after reassurance. He is enforcing a rule he believes the household should follow.

Function: monitoring and correction maintain control over a valued standard.

Again, neither brief case proves a diagnosis.

Case 6: The Moral Rule

Mei

Mei remembers a joke she made years ago and suddenly fears it proves she is a cruel person. She mentally reconstructs the event, searches her memory for the other person's expression, and asks friends whether they think the joke was offensive. No answer settles the question.

Possible OCD process: intrusive moral doubt and mental/reassurance compulsions.

Rafael

Rafael believes people who arrive late are disrespectful. He applies the rule rigidly, even when there are reasonable explanations. He ends a friendship after repeated lateness and says exceptions encourage irresponsibility.

Possible OCPD process: inflexible standard around morality or conscientiousness, if part of a broader clinically significant pattern.

Cultural caution

Values are shaped by culture, community, religion, family, and lived experience. A clinician should not treat disagreement with their own values as evidence of pathology.

The diagnostic issue is inflexibility and impairment in context.

Case 7: The Vacation

Maya

Before a trip, Maya repeatedly searches the route because she fears choosing a dangerous road. She asks her partner to confirm the route, checks crash statistics, and considers cancelling. Reassurance brings relief that does not last.

Marcus

Marcus plans every day of a vacation in thirty-minute blocks. When rain closes a museum, he spends the morning trying to reconstruct the schedule rather than choosing another activity. He becomes angry when his family wants an unplanned afternoon.

One pattern is organized around threat and certainty.

The other is organized around plan, order, and control.

A person can have both.

Case 8: The "Just Right" Desk

Nadia

Nadia adjusts objects on her desk until an internal feeling of wrongness settles. She does not believe the arrangement is objectively superior. In fact, she finds the repetition embarrassing. If she resists, the incompleteness becomes hard to tolerate.

That can fit an OCD "just right" or incompleteness process.

Elena

Elena has a preferred desk layout because she believes it is efficient. She expects shared desks to follow the same layout and corrects coworkers who change it. She can stop arranging once the system matches her standard, but she has difficulty tolerating someone else's system even when it works.

That can fit an OCPD-style standard and control pattern.

The two scenes look unusually similar.

Stance and function create the distinction.

Case 9: The Expense

Ben

Ben reviews a small credit-card purchase repeatedly because he fears it may be fraudulent and that failing to catch fraud means he was irresponsible. He checks the merchant name, searches the address, then checks again after doubt returns.

Theo

Theo objects to his partner buying an inexpensive item because he has strict rules about discretionary spending. He has adequate savings but treats small deviations from the plan as serious failures of discipline. He maintains similar rigid rules in other parts of life.

Financial behavior can appear in both patterns and in many other problems.

The fact that someone is cautious with money tells you very little without context.

Case 10: The Therapy Homework

Sofia

Sofia completes an ERP exercise, then asks the therapist whether she did it correctly. She worries that she accidentally performed a subtle compulsion. The therapist answers. Sofia feels relief, then identifies another detail and asks again.

The treatment task has become a new source of obsessional doubt.

Rafael

Rafael completes every therapy worksheet perfectly but resists exercises that ask him to permit another person to choose a method. He argues that the therapist is encouraging lower standards and brings detailed evidence that his system is more efficient.

The treatment relationship may be encountering the same rigidity present elsewhere.

This is one reason process matters inside therapy, not only outside it.

How to Use the Casebook

Do not ask which person you "are."

Choose one pair and ask which distinctions help you describe your own example more precisely.

Then write your example without a diagnosis label.

A clinician can do more with a clean sequence than with a character match.

Appendix F: Frequently Asked Questions

Is OCPD a Type of OCD?

No. They are separate diagnostic conditions.

OCD is characterized by obsessions, compulsions, or both. OCPD is a personality disorder characterized by a pervasive pattern involving order, perfectionism, and control. The names are similar, and the conditions can co-occur, but one is not simply a personality version or a more severe version of the other (Pinto et al., 2022).

The practical consequence is that a clinician should not infer OCPD from the severity of OCD or infer OCD from the intensity of perfectionism. Each pattern needs its own assessment.

Can Someone Have Both OCD and OCPD?

Yes. The conditions are not mutually exclusive, and clinical literature addresses presentations in which both are present (Wheaton et al., 2022).

If you see a clear obsession-compulsion loop alongside a broad, longstanding pattern of perfectionism, rigidity, or control, do not force all behavior into one column. Bring both patterns to the assessment.

Does OCD Always Involve Germs or Cleaning?

No.

Contamination is a well-known theme, but OCD can center on harm, responsibility, morality, religion, relationships, health, sexual themes, symmetry, incompleteness, mistakes, or other concerns. Compulsions can also be mental rather than visible.

If your home is untidy, that does not rule out OCD. The diagnostic question concerns obsessions, compulsions, distress, time, and impairment, not housekeeping style (National Institute of Mental Health, 2023).

Does OCPD Mean Someone Is Extremely Neat?

No.

Order can be part of the pattern, but OCPD is broader. Clinical descriptions include perfectionism that interferes with completion, excessive work focus, rigidity, difficulty delegating, and other patterns of control or inflexibility (Zimmerman, 2026).

A neat room is not a personality-disorder assessment.

If I Know a Fear Is Irrational, Does That Prove OCD?

No.

Recognizing that a fear is unlikely can be consistent with OCD, but insight varies. The diagnosis depends on the broader obsession-compulsion pattern and clinical criteria (American Psychiatric Association, 2022).

The more useful observation is what happens after the fear appears. Do you perform a ritual, mental review, avoidance behavior, or reassurance sequence that reduces distress temporarily?

If I Think My Standards Are Correct, Does That Prove OCPD?

No.

Defending a standard can be a useful clue to stance, particularly when the pattern is broad and longstanding. It does not prove a disorder.

People defend standards for cultural, moral, occupational, practical, and personal reasons. A clinician examines flexibility, reach, impairment, history, and alternative explanations.

Can OCD Look Like Perfectionism?

Yes.

A person may repeatedly check, revise, arrange, or seek a "just right" feeling because the behavior is part of an OCD loop. The perfectionistic appearance does not tell you the function.

Ask what would happen if the person stopped. Fear, guilt, uncertainty, or incompleteness may be central. The task is to identify the maintaining process.

Can OCPD Include Anxiety?

Yes. A person with OCPD can experience anxiety, and other anxiety disorders can co-occur.

Anxiety itself does not distinguish OCD from OCPD. The Five-Lens Difference Map asks what triggers the episode, what the person believes about it, what the response accomplishes, how broad the pattern is, and which treatment mechanism fits.

Is Reassurance Seeking Always OCD?

No.

Reassurance seeking can function as a compulsion in OCD, but people seek reassurance for many reasons. Relationship anxiety, health anxiety, trauma, ordinary uncertainty, and other problems can involve repeated questions.

Look for the loop: reassurance brings short-term relief, then the doubt returns and requests another answer.

Is Correcting Other People Always OCPD?

No.

People correct others because of job responsibilities, safety requirements, cultural expectations, irritability, expertise, anxiety, or simple disagreement.

For OCPD, a clinician looks for a broad, persistent, inflexible pattern of standards and control that creates impairment or distress, not one annoying habit.

Is Difficulty Delegating Specific to OCPD?

No.

Difficulty delegating is associated with OCPD, particularly when the person insists that others follow their exact method. It can also occur because of anxiety, lack of trust in a particular team, poor organizational systems, trauma, responsibility fears, or real competence problems.

The useful question is whether competent alternatives are tolerated and why they are not.

Can Someone With OCPD Know Their Behavior Is Causing Problems?

Yes.

The simplistic phrase "people with OCPD think everything is fine" is inaccurate. A person may recognize relationship damage, exhaustion, missed deadlines, or distress while still believing that the underlying standard is reasonable.

Separate stance toward the rule from feelings about its consequences.

Does OCPD Cause Intrusive Thoughts?

OCPD is not defined by the true obsessions and compulsions that characterize OCD. A person with OCPD can still have distressing thoughts for many reasons, and they can also have co-occurring OCD.

If recurrent intrusive, unwanted thoughts are followed by compulsive responses, those symptoms deserve direct assessment rather than being absorbed into a personality label.

If ERP Helped Me, Does That Prove I Have OCD?

No.

A treatment response can support a formulation, but it is not a standalone diagnostic test. Symptoms can change for many reasons, and interventions can affect more than one process.

A clinician should interpret response together with the original symptoms, treatment target, dose, adherence, other conditions, and functional change.

If ERP Did Not Help Me, Does That Prove I Have OCPD?

No.

Nonresponse can reflect an incomplete formulation, covert compulsions, insufficient treatment, poor delivery, comorbidity, another condition, or many other factors.

Treat "this did not change" as useful information. Ask why the treatment was expected to work and what should be reconsidered.

Is ERP an OCPD Treatment?

ERP is an established OCD treatment. OCPD has a smaller treatment evidence base, and clinical reviews discuss other psychotherapeutic approaches rather than an established OCPD-specific ERP protocol (Pinto et al., 2022).

A clinician may use exposure or behavioral experiments within an individualized plan for many reasons. That is different from saying OCPD is treated with the same standard ERP protocol as OCD.

Can Medication Tell the Conditions Apart?

No.

Medication can be used in OCD care. The randomized medication evidence for OCPD is limited (Gecaite-Stonciene et al., 2022).

Improvement or nonimprovement after a medication does not establish a diagnosis.

What if My Symptoms Changed Over Time?

Tell the clinician.

OCD severity and themes can change. A personality pattern can also be experienced differently as relationships, work, age, therapy, and circumstances change.

A timeline is useful because it separates longstanding features from new symptoms. Sudden or major changes in personality or behavior can also have medical or other causes that require professional evaluation.

What if I Cannot Remember When the Pattern Began?

Use broad periods and say what you do not know.

Do not construct false precision. A clinician may use collateral history, records, or repeated assessment when developmental timing matters.

"I remember this clearly by my first job, but I am unsure about adolescence" is better than a guessed age.

What if My Partner Thinks I Have OCPD?

Treat their observation as one source of information, not a diagnosis.

Ask them for specific examples: what happens, how often, how the pattern affects them, and where else they see it.

A partner may notice Reach and interpersonal cost very clearly. They may not know the internal trigger or function unless you discuss it.

What if My Partner Thinks I Have OCD?

The same rule applies.

Ask what they observe. If they notice repeated reassurance, checking, avoidance, or rituals, those examples can be useful in an assessment.

Do not let the relationship become a diagnostic contest.

What if My Clinician Has Never Mentioned OCPD?

You can ask directly.

> *I have a longstanding pattern of perfectionism, control, and difficulty delegating that does not seem connected to my intrusive fears. Is OCPD or another personality pattern worth assessing?*

A qualified clinician may explain why it does or does not fit. The value is in having the differential considered, not obtaining a preferred label.

What if My Clinician Has Never Mentioned OCD?

Describe the loop.

> *I get recurrent unwanted thoughts, and I respond with repeated checking and mental review that reduce distress briefly. Could OCD be part of the differential?*

Specific sequences are easier to assess than a self-applied label.

Could Autism or ADHD Explain Some of This?

Possibly. Rigidity, routines, perfectionism, executive-function difficulties, sensory needs, hyperfocus, and repetitive behavior can appear in neurodevelopmental conditions. Anxiety, trauma, depression, eating disorders, and other conditions can also overlap with parts of the picture.

This volume is deliberately narrow. If the Five-Lens Difference Map does not explain an important pattern, that is a reason to widen the assessment rather than force a binary answer.

What if I Am Afraid of Getting the Diagnosis "Wrong"?

That fear is understandable, especially if you have already spent years under one label.

Try changing the goal from "get the right label immediately" to "make the important patterns visible."

A good assessment can tolerate uncertainty, revision, and more than one condition. Your one-page summary should make the question clearer without requiring you to solve it before the appointment.

Appendix G: A Thirty-Day Observation Journal

These pages turn Chapter 15 into a printable working section.

The journal is intentionally repetitive because the purpose is comparison across time. Keep entries short. If recording becomes compulsive, reduce the frequency and discuss that pattern with your clinician.

Days 1 to 7: Trigger, Response, Immediate Effect

Day 1

Situation or trigger:

What I did next:

What changed immediately:

Time or relationship cost:

Day 2

Situation or trigger:

What I did next:

What changed immediately:

Time or relationship cost:

Day 3

Situation or trigger:

What I did next:

What changed immediately:

Time or relationship cost:

Day 4

Situation or trigger:

What I did next:

What changed immediately:

Time or relationship cost:

Day 5

Situation or trigger:

What I did next:

What changed immediately:

Time or relationship cost:

Day 6

Situation or trigger:

What I did next:

What changed immediately:

Time or relationship cost:

Day 7

Situation or trigger:

What I did next:

What changed immediately:

Time or relationship cost:

Week 1 Review

Choose one pattern. Do not analyze all seven entries.

Repeated trigger:

Repeated response:

Repeated immediate effect:

Question this raises:

Days 8 to 14: Add Stance

For each day, describe your relationship to the thought, rule, urge, or standard in ordinary words.

Day 8

Trigger:

Thought, rule, urge, or standard:

How it felt to me:

Response:

Immediate effect:

Day 9

Trigger:

Thought, rule, urge, or standard:

How it felt to me:

Response:

Immediate effect:

Day 10

Trigger:

Thought, rule, urge, or standard:

How it felt to me:

Response:

Immediate effect:

Day 11

Trigger:

Thought, rule, urge, or standard:

How it felt to me:

Response:

Immediate effect:

Day 12

Trigger:

Thought, rule, urge, or standard:

How it felt to me:

Response:

Immediate effect:

Day 13

Trigger:

Thought, rule, urge, or standard:

How it felt to me:

Response:

Immediate effect:

Day 14

Trigger:

Thought, rule, urge, or standard:

How it felt to me:

Response:

Immediate effect:

Week 2 Review

Choose one entry.

Did I want the thought or rule?

Did I believe it was true or correct?

Did I believe acting on it was necessary?

Did I dislike the rule, the consequence, or both?

What happened if I resisted, delayed, or was prevented from responding?

Days 15 to 21: Reach

Use one life domain per day.

Day 15: Work or School

Repeated fear/doubt loop:

Repeated standards/control pattern:

How long I remember this pattern:

Main cost:

Day 16: Home

Repeated fear/doubt loop:

Repeated standards/control pattern:

How long I remember this pattern:

Main cost:

Day 17: Close Relationships

Repeated fear/doubt loop:

Repeated standards/control pattern:

How long I remember this pattern:

Main cost:

Day 18: Money and Possessions

Repeated fear/doubt loop:

Repeated standards/control pattern:

How long I remember this pattern:

Main cost:

Day 19: Health and Safety

Repeated fear/doubt loop:

Repeated standards/control pattern:

How long I remember this pattern:

Main cost:

Day 20: Travel and Plans

Repeated fear/doubt loop:

Repeated standards/control pattern:

How long I remember this pattern:

Main cost:

Day 21: Rest and Leisure

Repeated fear/doubt loop:

Repeated standards/control pattern:

How long I remember this pattern:

Main cost:

Week 3 Review

Which pattern is narrowest?

Which pattern is broadest?

Which pattern appears to be most longstanding?

Which area does not fit either explanation well?

Days 22 to 28: Treatment Fit

If you are not in treatment, use these days to review past treatment or prepare questions for an assessment.

Day 22: Current Formulation

What diagnosis or explanation is currently being used?

What does it explain well?

What does it explain poorly?

Day 23: Target

What behavior is treatment trying to change?

How was that target selected?

Day 24: Maintaining Process

What do I think maintains the behavior?

What does my clinician think maintains it?

Where do our explanations differ?

Day 25: Treatment Mechanism

What is the intervention supposed to change?

Can I explain that link in one sentence?

Day 26: Response

What improved?

What did not improve?

What new information did the response provide?

Day 27: Mismatch

What part of the plan feels mismatched?

Is it difficult but relevant, or genuinely unclear in mechanism?

Day 28: Review Question

What one question would make the treatment logic clearer?

Day 29: One-Page Summary Draft

Current question:

Pattern A:

Pattern B:

Reach and timeline:

Functional cost:

Treatment history:

Question 1:

Question 2:

Question 3:

Stop.

Day 30: Appointment Preparation

My opening sentence:

The one example I most want to discuss:

The one contradiction I do not want to hide:

What I want explained about treatment fit:

What I will do if the answer is uncertain:

The final line might simply be: "Ask what information would make the next review more useful."

Appendix H: Other Explanations to Keep Open

A book called *Is It OCPD or OCD?* has a built-in risk. It can make the reader look at every rigid, repetitive, perfectionistic, or anxious behavior and assume the answer must be one of two diagnoses.

Clinical assessment is wider than a book title.

This appendix is not a second diagnostic manual. It is a reminder of what the Five-Lens Difference Map cannot settle.

Ordinary Personality and Conscientiousness

People differ in conscientiousness, orderliness, thrift, persistence, and preference for routine.

A trait becomes clinically relevant only in context. A person who likes clear systems, prefers careful work, and dislikes clutter does not have OCPD simply because those traits are strong.

Ask about flexibility and cost.

Can the person adapt when the situation changes? Can they accept another competent method? Does the standard repeatedly defeat the task's purpose or damage relationships?

Clinical significance matters.

General Anxiety and Worry

Generalized worry can involve repeated thinking, reassurance, checking, and difficulty tolerating uncertainty.

The distinction from OCD can require careful assessment of the nature of intrusive experiences, compulsions, and the broader anxiety pattern.

Do not assume that every repeated worry is an obsession or every coping behavior is a compulsion.

Illness Anxiety and Health Concerns

Repeated body checking, medical research, reassurance, and fear can occur in OCD, illness anxiety, medical conditions, or ordinary responses to health uncertainty.

Real symptoms require appropriate medical assessment.

The Five-Lens Difference Map can describe the sequence, but it cannot determine whether a physical concern is medically benign.

Depression

Depression can change motivation, decision-making, concentration, self-criticism, and the ability to experience rest or pleasure.

A person may become stuck on mistakes because their mood is low. They may withdraw from relationships. They may appear inflexible because cognitive and emotional resources are depleted.

If mood symptoms are substantial, include them in the assessment rather than treating them as background noise.

Trauma-Related Patterns

Trauma can shape threat monitoring, safety behavior, control, avoidance, and difficulty trusting other people.

A rigid routine may function as an attempt to maintain safety after chaos.

Repeated checking may be linked to hypervigilance rather than an OCD compulsion.

A clinician needs the context to distinguish these possibilities.

Autism

Autistic people can have strong routines, sensory preferences, focused interests, a need for predictability, or distress around unexpected change. Some autistic people also have OCD, and personality-disorder differentials can be complicated.

The internal reason for sameness, the developmental history, sensory factors, social communication, and broader neurodevelopmental profile all matter.

Do not interpret a preference for sameness as OCPD without considering neurodevelopmental context.

ADHD

ADHD can produce missed deadlines, inconsistent organization, repeated checking to compensate for forgetfulness, hyperfocus, time-management problems, and shame-driven overpreparation.

A person may build rigid systems because they are trying to compensate for executive-function difficulties.

The presence of a detailed system does not reveal why the system exists.

Eating Disorders

Perfectionism, rigid rules, checking, and ritualized behavior can appear in eating disorders. OCD can co-occur with eating disorders, and OCPD traits may also be present.

When food, weight, body image, or exercise are central, specialized assessment is important.

Other Personality Patterns

Rigidity, conflict, sensitivity to criticism, interpersonal control, and perfectionism can appear in several personality configurations.

OCPD should not become a catch-all label for a difficult person.

Personality assessment looks at the full pattern, developmental history, functioning, and differential diagnoses.

Occupational Culture

Some jobs require meticulous checking, strict procedures, documentation, and low tolerance for error.

The same behavior that looks excessive in one setting may be mandatory in another.

Aviation, medicine, laboratory work, regulated finance, cybersecurity, and other fields can have legitimate multi-step checking processes.

Ask whether the behavior exceeds the real standard and whether it persists in low-stakes settings.

Family and Cultural Rules

People inherit beliefs about money, cleanliness, time, work, religion, respect, and responsibility.

A clinician should understand those norms before calling a behavior inflexible or excessive.

The question is not whether a person differs from the clinician.

The question is whether the pattern is maladaptive in the person's cultural and relational context.

Medical and Neurological Causes

Significant new changes in personality, cognition, behavior, or anxiety can have medical causes.

If a pattern appears suddenly, especially with confusion, neurological symptoms, medication changes, substance use, or other physical changes, professional medical assessment may be important.

A longstanding personality diagnosis should not be used to explain away an abrupt change.

Substance Use and Medication Effects

Substances and medications can affect anxiety, sleep, attention, mood, inhibition, and behavior.

Include relevant use and medication changes in the history you give a clinician.

Do not change prescribed medication based on this book.

The Wide-Lens Question

When the OCPD versus OCD comparison feels too neat, ask:

What important feature of my experience does neither explanation account for?

That question protects the assessment from tunnel vision.

The best differential process is not the one that gives you the fastest label.

It is the one that leaves fewer important facts unexplained.

Appendix I: Pattern Bank for Practice

The fastest way to learn the Five-Lens Difference Map is to practice on examples where the answer is not supplied.

Each vignette below is deliberately incomplete. Read it, then ask what information is missing. That is how a real differential works.

Pattern 1: The Receipt

Daniel keeps every receipt and organizes them by month. He becomes uncomfortable when his partner throws one away.

What is missing?

You do not know whether Daniel fears a specific financial catastrophe, whether the receipts are part of a compulsion, whether he has rigid record-keeping standards across many domains, whether there is a real tax or business reason to keep them, or whether the behavior causes impairment.

Useful next questions:

What does he think will happen if a receipt is discarded? Does keeping it reduce a recurring fear? Does he insist that other people follow the same system? How broad and longstanding is the pattern?

Pattern 2: The Presentation

Maya practices a presentation twenty times.

The number is not enough.

She may be preparing for a high-stakes event. She may have social anxiety. She may be neutralizing obsessional doubt about saying something harmful. She may believe that a professional presentation should be flawless. She may have both an OCD loop and a broad perfectionistic style.

Ask what makes the twenty-first rehearsal feel necessary.

Pattern 3: The Bedtime Routine

Ben follows the same bedtime routine every night and becomes distressed when it is interrupted.

Possible explanations include OCD, an autistic need for predictability, insomnia-management habits, trauma-related safety behavior, OCPD-style rules, or an ordinary routine.

The key missing information includes what the routine is meant to accomplish, whether there are obsessions or compulsions, whether the rule is defended as correct, and what else is present developmentally.

Pattern 4: The Driving Route

Elena insists on taking the same route to work even when traffic is worse.

If she fears that another route will cause an accident and repeatedly checks traffic reports to obtain certainty, an OCD process might be relevant.

If she believes the known route is the proper, efficient system and rejects alternatives despite evidence, broader rigidity may be relevant.

If she is avoiding a road where she experienced a traumatic collision, a trauma formulation may be more important.

The route does not identify the mechanism.

Pattern 5: The Rewritten Chore

Marcus asks his teenager to clean the bathroom. Afterward, he cleans it again.

A photograph shows one person redoing another person's work.

The Five-Lens Difference Map asks why.

Did Marcus fear contamination? Did he experience an intolerable "not right" feeling? Did he think the teenager's method violated a household standard? Was the bathroom actually not clean? Does Marcus repeat this across nearly every delegated task?

Each answer changes the question.

Pattern 6: The Health Search

Sofia spends two hours searching a symptom online.

This could be an OCD reassurance or checking loop, illness anxiety, a response to a real medical problem, ordinary research after a new symptom, or another process.

Ask whether searching settles the concern. If relief lasts only minutes and another query immediately appears, the behavior may be functioning as repetitive reassurance.

A health question that remains medically unresolved still deserves appropriate professional care.

Pattern 7: The Shared Calendar

Rafael builds a shared calendar for the family and becomes angry when other people add events without following his color system.

The color system is not clinically important.

The rigidity might be.

Ask whether the system serves a real coordination need, whether different competent systems are tolerated, how conflict is handled, and whether similar rules govern other shared tasks.

Pattern 8: The Apology

Nadia apologizes to a friend three times for the same small comment.

If each apology is an attempt to obtain certainty that she is not a bad person, with relief that quickly fades, the sequence could fit a moral OCD loop.

If Nadia has a rigid moral code and insists others make the same repeated apologies after minor breaches, a broader standards pattern might also deserve assessment.

If the friend actually asked for clarification after a serious harm, context changes again.

Pattern 9: The Savings Rule

Theo refuses to spend money on leisure despite having adequate savings.

OCPD descriptions include restrictive approaches to spending, but one behavior is not enough.

Ask whether Theo has a longstanding belief that money must be reserved for future emergencies, how flexible the rule is, whether financial history explains it, and whether the pattern is part of broader rigidity.

Also ask whether spending triggers intrusive catastrophic fears followed by checking or reassurance.

Pattern 10: The Deleted File

Priya cannot delete old digital files.

A simplistic checklist might call this hoarding or OCPD.

A better assessment asks why.

Does she fear losing information she may need? Does deletion trigger responsibility obsessions? Does she believe organized archives are objectively necessary? Is storage unlimited and harmless, or is the behavior causing real impairment? Does she have broader difficulty discarding physical items?

One behavior can touch several differentials.

Pattern 11: The Food Preparation Rule

Aisha refuses to let anyone else prepare a particular meal because they do not follow her sequence.

If contamination fears and washing rituals drive the sequence, OCD may be relevant.

If Aisha believes there is one correct culinary method and applies similar standards across many tasks, OCPD traits may be relevant.

If the sequence is required for a family member's severe allergy, it may be appropriate.

The safety context comes before the psychology.

Pattern 12: The Draft Folder

Lucas has forty-seven unsent email drafts.

Why?

He may avoid sending because of obsessional fear of causing offense.

He may be unable to consider the wording sufficiently polished.

He may have ADHD and start messages without finishing them.

He may be overwhelmed by workload.

Count is less useful than sequence.

Pattern 13: The Meeting Notes

Mei writes exhaustive meeting notes and corrects colleagues' summaries.

If she fears forgetting a detail that could cause harm and repeatedly reviews notes, OCD might be relevant.

If she thinks her documentation standard is the only responsible one and insists others follow it, OCPD features might be relevant.

If she works in a regulated setting where detailed notes are required, the behavior may be entirely appropriate.

Pattern 14: The Relationship Question

Jordan asks every day whether he loves his partner enough.

The content sounds like indecision.

A possible OCD pattern would involve intrusive doubt, mental checking of feelings, comparison, reassurance, and temporary relief.

A different pattern could involve ordinary relationship uncertainty, depression, attachment difficulties, or another issue.

OCPD is not automatically relevant because the person wants certainty.

Pattern 15: The Corrected Story

Rafael interrupts his partner to correct small factual details while she tells a story.

The behavior may reflect a broad need for accuracy and correctness. It may also reflect social communication style, anxiety, habit, competitiveness, or relationship dynamics.

Ask whether the correction is hard to resist because a thought feels incomplete, whether factual precision is treated as a rule across contexts, and what happens when Rafael deliberately lets a harmless inaccuracy pass.

Pattern 16: The Repeated Prayer

Sofia repeats a prayer until it feels "right."

If she is trying to neutralize intrusive blasphemous thoughts or achieve a sense of moral certainty, the act may be a compulsion.

Religious practice itself is not pathology. A clinician must understand what is normative in the person's faith community and what is driven by distressing repetitive processes beyond those norms.

OCPD can also involve inflexible moral standards, but content alone cannot distinguish the two.

Pattern 17: The Packing List

Maya starts packing a week before a trip and uses a detailed list.

Ordinary.

Then imagine she restarts packing repeatedly because she fears forgetting one item will cause catastrophe.

Possible OCD process.

Now imagine she requires every family member to use her list, rejects substitutions, and treats spontaneous changes as irresponsibility.

Possible broad control pattern.

Now imagine she has a disability that makes forgotten medication dangerous.

Context changes the meaning again.

Pattern 18: The Checked Child

Ben checks on his sleeping child six times.

A new parent may reasonably check frequently.

An OCD pattern might include intrusive fears of accidental death, repeated checking beyond realistic safety needs, and temporary relief that quickly fails.

An OCPD pattern is less obvious from this behavior unless it belongs to a broader system of rigid parenting standards and control.

Do not use a count without developmental and safety context.

Pattern 19: The Project Takeover

Elena delegates a project, then takes it back halfway through.

The first question is whether the employee was actually failing.

If not, ask what Elena could not tolerate.

A fear of being responsible for an unnoticed mistake may suggest obsessional responsibility.

A conviction that only her method meets the standard may suggest OCPD-style control.

Fear of being blamed by an abusive manager points toward the environment.

Pattern 20: The Book About OCD and OCPD

A reader highlights every sentence in this book, rereads the comparisons, and keeps asking whether the examples "really" fit.

The content of the book does not protect it from becoming part of a compulsive search for certainty.

If reading provides temporary reassurance followed by renewed doubt, consider closing the book and bringing the pattern itself to a clinician.

If the reader is instead building a detailed taxonomy because they believe the distinctions must be perfectly organized before they can speak to a clinician, perfectionistic control may be part of the process.

If they are simply studying carefully, there may be no clinical problem at all.

The useful question remains the same: what job is the behavior doing?

Appendix J: What a Good Differential Assessment Tries to Answer

A reader can arrive prepared and still not know what a clinician is doing with the information.

This appendix explains the logic of a differential assessment without prescribing how any specific professional should practice.

The Assessment Starts Wider Than Two Labels

A careful assessment does not begin with the assumption that the answer must be OCD or OCPD.

The clinician usually needs to understand the presenting problem, history, severity, impairment, medical context, substance use, medications, developmental factors, mood, anxiety, trauma, neurodevelopmental features, and other relevant conditions.

The exact scope depends on the setting and clinician.

Your job as a patient is not to conduct that entire assessment yourself.

Your job is to report important facts accurately.

The Clinician Looks for the Core Pattern

For OCD, the clinician needs to understand whether there are obsessions, compulsions, or both, and whether the pattern reaches a clinically significant threshold. They will want to know what thoughts or experiences are intrusive, what responses follow, how much time the cycle takes, how much distress or impairment it causes, and whether another condition or substance better explains it (American Psychiatric Association, 2022).

For OCPD, the clinician looks for a broad, enduring pattern involving order, perfectionism, and control, together with characteristic forms of rigidity and functional or interpersonal cost. Developmental timing and cross-situational reach are important because a personality disorder is not defined by one recent behavior (Zimmerman, 2026).

The Five-Lens Difference Map was designed around these different kinds of pattern.

The Clinician Separates Content From Process

Two people can worry about contamination.

One may have recurrent intrusive contamination obsessions and washing compulsions.

Another may have rigid household cleanliness standards they view as correct.

A third may have a medical vulnerability that makes contamination precautions reasonable.

A fourth may have trauma linked to illness.

The content word *contamination* does not finish the assessment.

Process, history, and context do.

The Clinician Asks About Impairment

Symptoms and traits become diagnostically important partly through their consequences.

Impairment can involve time, work, school, relationships, health, sleep, avoidance, distress, and lost opportunity.

OCPD presents a particular challenge because some traits may be rewarded or experienced as strengths. The assessment should still ask whether inflexibility and perfectionism create meaningful costs.

Likewise, OCD can be hidden by success. A person may maintain employment while spending several private hours a day on rituals.

Functioning needs detail.

The Clinician Considers Insight Without Making It a Gate

In OCD, insight can vary. That means the clinician should not rule out OCD simply because a person is highly convinced by an obsessional belief (American Psychiatric Association, 2022).

In OCPD, standards and control patterns are often experienced as consistent with the person's values or preferred way of doing things, but awareness of consequences can still be substantial.

A good assessment asks what the person believes, how strongly they believe it, how that changes across time, and what happens when the pattern is challenged.

The Clinician Looks for More Than One Process

A patient may have contamination OCD and longstanding OCPD traits.

They may have OCD and autism.

They may have OCPD and depression.

They may have one diagnosis plus ordinary personality traits.

The assessment should not force every problem into the first label identified.

This is especially important after treatment begins. If one symptom cluster improves and another remains unchanged, the unchanged pattern may need a separate formulation.

The Clinician Uses Treatment History Carefully

A history of ERP can be informative.

If well-delivered ERP clearly reduced obsession-compulsion symptoms, that supports the usefulness of the OCD formulation for those symptoms.

It does not prove that every remaining behavior is OCD.

If ERP did not help, the clinician should ask what treatment was actually delivered, whether compulsions were accurately identified, whether covert rituals continued, whether the dose was adequate, whether comorbid conditions affected treatment, and whether the formulation needs review.

Treatment history is evidence with context.

The Clinician May Use Structured Measures

Mental health professionals sometimes use structured interviews, symptom scales, or personality measures to support assessment.

A scale can organize information and track severity.

It does not replace clinical judgment.

This is another reason the worksheets in this book are deliberately unscored. They are preparation tools, not substitutes for validated assessment methods.

The Clinician Should Be Able to Explain the Formulation

You may not agree with every conclusion, but you should be able to ask what the clinician thinks is happening.

A useful explanation connects:

the trigger,

the meaning,

the response,

the maintaining process,

the broader history,

and the treatment target.

For example:

"Your driving problem looks like OCD because an intrusive harm doubt triggers repeated checking and reassurance, which briefly reduces anxiety and then strengthens the cycle. ERP targets the checking and avoidance."

Or:

"The broader work and relationship pattern looks different. The standards and delegation problems have been present for many years, are defended as correct, and extend beyond obsessional themes. We should assess personality features separately."

That is a formulation.

What a Differential Assessment Does Not Promise

It does not promise perfect certainty.

Diagnoses can change when more information becomes available.

Symptoms can overlap.

Research can be incomplete.

A person's presentation can evolve.

A competent clinician may say that one diagnosis is likely, another is possible, and further observation is needed.

Uncertainty is not always a sign of poor care.

The question is whether the uncertainty is being managed thoughtfully.

Red Flags in the Reasoning Process

No single sentence proves that an assessment is poor, but some statements deserve follow-up.

"OCD just means being neat."

"OCPD is simply severe OCD."

"You cannot have both."

"If you know the thought is irrational, it is OCD, and if you do not, it is OCPD."

"ERP did not work, so it cannot be OCD."

"You are successful at work, so this cannot be impairing."

"You disagree with me, so that proves OCPD."

Each statement oversimplifies a more complex clinical question.

Ask for the reasoning underneath.

What to Do With a Good Assessment

Write down the formulation in plain language.

Ask which symptoms belong to which process.

Ask how treatment targets follow.

Ask what outcome will be tracked.

Ask what would trigger review.

Then return to ordinary life.

The point of assessment is not to spend every day monitoring diagnostic identity. It is to make care more accurate and life more workable.

Appendix K: Four Reusable Clinician-Ready Worksheets

The following four copies are intentionally identical. Use one for each pattern you want to discuss. Four is a limit, not a target.

Pattern Sheet 1

Concrete behavior:

Trigger:

Thought, image, urge, rule, or standard:

How I relate to it:

Response:

Immediate effect:

How long the effect lasts:

Where else this appears:

How long I remember it:

Concrete cost:

What treatment has targeted it, if any:

What I do not understand:

Question for clinician:

Pattern Sheet 2

Concrete behavior:

Trigger:

Thought, image, urge, rule, or standard:

How I relate to it:

Response:

Immediate effect:

How long the effect lasts:

Where else this appears:

How long I remember it:

Concrete cost:

What treatment has targeted it, if any:

What I do not understand:

Question for clinician:

Pattern Sheet 3

Concrete behavior:

Trigger:

Thought, image, urge, rule, or standard:

How I relate to it:

Response:

Immediate effect:

How long the effect lasts:

Where else this appears:

How long I remember it:

Concrete cost:

What treatment has targeted it, if any:

What I do not understand:

Question for clinician:

Pattern Sheet 4

Concrete behavior:

Trigger:

Thought, image, urge, rule, or standard:

How I relate to it:

Response:

Immediate effect:

How long the effect lasts:

Where else this appears:

How long I remember it:

Concrete cost:

What treatment has targeted it, if any:

What I do not understand:

Question for clinician:

Appendix L: Ten Mistakes That Make the Differential Harder

The OCPD and OCD differential becomes less accurate when a useful clue is promoted into a complete rule.

These ten mistakes are worth reviewing before a diagnostic appointment because each one can distort the story you tell.

Mistake 1: Starting With Neatness

Neatness is visually memorable and clinically weak.

A tidy kitchen does not establish OCD. A messy kitchen does not rule it out. An organized desk does not establish OCPD.

Start with a costly episode instead.

If a person repeatedly cleans because intrusive contamination fears are followed by washing that briefly reduces distress, the sequence is relevant to OCD.

If a person enforces organization as a broad, inflexible standard across home and work, OCPD may be part of the differential.

If a person simply likes order and can be flexible when needed, neither disorder may apply.

The correction is simple: **describe function before appearance**.

Mistake 2: Treating "Ego-Dystonic Versus Ego-Syntonic" as a Test

The distinction between unwanted experiences and endorsed standards is important.

It is not sufficient.

OCD insight varies, and people with OCPD can recognize painful consequences or become ambivalent about longstanding patterns. A person may also have one ego-dystonic pattern and another ego-syntonic pattern.

The correction is to separate questions:

Do I want the thought?

Do I believe it?

Do I think the rule is correct?

Do I think the behavior is necessary?

Do I dislike the pattern, the consequences, or both?

Then add function and reach.

Mistake 3: Assuming Every Repeated Behavior Is a Compulsion

Repetition is not the defining feature of a compulsion.

People repeat behavior because they are learning, practicing, following procedure, compensating for memory problems, pursuing a standard, responding to a real risk, or trying to reduce obsessional distress.

The word *compulsion* should be connected to an OCD formulation, not used as a synonym for "something I do a lot."

If you say "I compulsively edit," be ready to describe what makes the editing compulsive.

What happens if you stop?

What does editing change?

Does the relief last?

What obsessional meaning is present?

If those questions do not fit, say "repeated editing" until a clinician helps formulate it.

Mistake 4: Assuming Every Standard Is OCPD

Strong standards occur everywhere.

A surgeon follows sterile procedure.

An accountant reconciles figures.

A musician practices details.

A parent enforces a safety rule.

A religious community has norms.

A person with no disorder may be highly conscientious.

OCPD requires a broader clinical pattern. Context, flexibility, duration, and impairment matter.

The correction is to ask whether the standard can bend when circumstances reasonably require it, whether it is imposed broadly on others, and whether it repeatedly defeats important goals.

Mistake 5: Using Treatment Response as Proof

"I improved with ERP, so every problem I have is OCD."

"ERP did not help, so I do not have OCD."

Both statements go too far.

Treatment response can be informative. It can also be affected by target selection, treatment quality, duration, hidden rituals, comorbidity, adherence, expectations, and other factors.

The correction is to connect response to a specific target.

"ERP reduced my contamination washing, but it did not change my longstanding difficulty delegating."

That sentence is clinically useful.

"ERP failed me" is too broad.

Mistake 6: Making the Differential a Moral Argument

OCD can burden partners through reassurance, avoidance, and rituals.

OCPD can burden partners through rigidity, criticism, and control.

Neither diagnosis decides who is a good person.

A partner can be harmed by a pattern and still misunderstand its function. A person can have a mental disorder and still be responsible for threatening, coercive, or abusive behavior.

The correction is to separate three questions:

What is happening clinically?

What impact is the behavior having?

What boundaries or safety actions are needed?

Do not use the diagnosis to erase any of the three.

Mistake 7: Hiding Evidence That Does Not Fit

People preparing for an assessment often become advocates for one answer.

They collect examples that support the preferred diagnosis and minimize contradictory ones.

This is understandable. It also makes differential diagnosis worse.

If you believe OCPD fits but you have recurrent unwanted thoughts followed by rituals and short-term relief, include that.

If you believe OCD fits but you have a broad, longstanding pattern of standards and control that you usually defend as correct, include that.

If neither label explains sensory overload, executive-function difficulties, trauma triggers, mood episodes, or another major feature, include that.

The correction is to bring the fact that is hardest for your preferred explanation to account for.

Mistake 8: Collecting Too Much Data

Self-observation can become a full-time activity.

For someone with OCD, it can also become a checking or reassurance process.

You do not need a transcript of your month.

A clinician can often learn more from two representative sequences than from sixty pages of notes.

The correction is to set limits.

One episode per day during observation.

One-page summary.

Three main questions.

Four pattern sheets at most.

If the urge to collect more feels difficult to resist, that urge may itself be worth discussing.

Mistake 9: Forgetting Time and Development

A pattern that began three months ago after a major stressor carries different information from one that has appeared across settings since early adulthood.

OCD can begin in childhood, adolescence, or adulthood and can change in theme and severity. Personality-disorder assessment also considers enduring patterns and developmental history.

The correction is not to produce an exact origin story.

Use broad periods.

"These control patterns were present in my first job and in college roommates' descriptions of me."

"The intrusive driving fears began after I became a parent."

"I cannot remember whether the rigidity was present before age eighteen."

Honest uncertainty is better than invented precision.

Mistake 10: Believing the Appointment Must End With Certainty

A differential assessment may end with a clear diagnosis.

It may also end with a working formulation, a provisional diagnosis, a request for more history, a structured assessment, or a plan to observe treatment response.

That is not necessarily failure.

The dangerous alternative is false certainty.

If the clinician says, "I think OCD is clear, but I want more information before deciding whether the broader personality pattern meets criteria for OCPD," you have learned something useful.

If they say, "The rigidity appears better explained by autism and occupational habits than by OCPD," ask how they reached that conclusion.

If they say, "I am not sure yet," ask what information would reduce the uncertainty.

The correction is to seek **clarity before certainty**.

A Final Pre-Appointment Check

Before you bring your notes to a clinician, read these seven statements.

I have described behaviors rather than relying on labels.

I have included triggers, stance, function, and reach.

I have included at least one fact that does not fit my preferred explanation.

I have described treatment response without treating it as proof.

I have named concrete costs.

I have kept other explanations open.

I have questions rather than a verdict.

If those statements are true, you are prepared enough.

The appointment can do the rest.

Appendix M: Plain-Language Glossary

The same words are used differently in everyday speech and clinical work. This glossary keeps the book's recurring terms consistent.

Avoidance

A behavior that keeps a person away from a feared, distressing, or difficult trigger.

In OCD, avoidance can reduce contact with obsessional triggers and can function like a safety strategy. It may make symptoms look quieter while preserving the underlying fear.

Avoidance also occurs in many other conditions, so the word does not identify a diagnosis.

Compulsion

A repetitive behavior or mental act that a person feels driven to perform, often in response to an obsession or according to rules that feel difficult not to follow. In OCD, compulsions commonly aim to reduce distress or prevent a feared event, even when they are excessive or not realistically connected to the outcome (American Psychiatric Association, 2022).

Compulsions can be visible or mental.

Comorbidity

The presence of more than one diagnosable condition in the same person.

For this book, the key implication is that OCD and OCPD are not mutually exclusive.

Comorbidity can make a presentation less tidy because one behavior may be influenced by more than one process.

Differential Diagnosis

The clinical process of distinguishing among conditions that could explain a person's symptoms or patterns.

A differential is not a popularity contest between labels. It asks which explanation best accounts for the full evidence and what alternatives should remain open.

Ego-Dystonic

A thought, urge, image, rule, or behavior experienced as inconsistent with a person's wishes, identity, or values.

OCD obsessions are often described this way because they can be intrusive and unwanted.

The term is a clue, not a diagnosis. Insight varies.

Ego-Syntonic

A thought, rule, standard, or behavior experienced as compatible with a person's values or self-concept.

OCPD traits are often described this way because standards and control may feel justified or correct.

A person can still dislike the consequences of an ego-syntonic pattern.

Exposure and Response Prevention

A form of cognitive behavioral treatment with strong evidence for OCD.

Exposure involves contact with feared or avoided triggers. Response prevention involves reducing the compulsive response that would usually be used to obtain relief or certainty. The treatment is individualized and is best understood through the specific OCD formulation (National Institute of Mental Health, 2023).

The abbreviation used in this book is **ERP**.

Five-Lens Difference Map

The observation framework used throughout this book.

The five lenses are Trigger, Stance, Function, Reach, and Treatment Fit.

The map does not diagnose. It organizes examples so a qualified clinician can assess them more clearly.

Function

What a behavior accomplishes in the immediate sequence.

Examples include reducing anxiety, obtaining reassurance, restoring a sense of order, enforcing a standard, avoiding uncertainty, or taking control of a task.

Function is not the same as moral motive.

Functional Impairment

The concrete effect a symptom or pattern has on a person's ability to work, study, maintain relationships, care for themselves, rest, participate in life, or meet other important demands.

Impairment can exist even when a person looks successful from the outside.

Insight

The degree to which a person recognizes that a belief, fear, symptom, or pattern may be inaccurate, excessive, or problematic.

In OCD, insight can vary. It should not be reduced to a yes-or-no question.

In OCPD, a person may defend a standard while still recognizing its costs.

Obsession

A recurrent and persistent thought, urge, or image experienced as intrusive and unwanted and commonly associated with anxiety or distress in OCD (American Psychiatric Association, 2022).

Everyday enthusiasm is not an obsession in this clinical sense.

OCPD Pattern

The phrase used in this book for a broad, enduring pattern of perfectionism, order, control, and rigidity that may warrant assessment for OCPD.

Using the phrase does not mean the person has the diagnosis.

It helps us describe features without assigning a label prematurely.

Reach

How widely a pattern extends across settings, relationships, roles, and time.

A behavior that occurs only around one obsessional theme has different Reach from a longstanding style that organizes work, home, money, delegation, and relationships.

Reach is one lens, not a standalone test.

Reassurance Seeking

Asking another person, a professional, a book, an internet search, or another source to provide certainty or reduce doubt.

In OCD, repeated reassurance can function as a compulsion when the relief is temporary and the question returns.

Ordinary requests for information are not automatically reassurance compulsions.

Stance

The person's relationship to a thought, rule, urge, or standard.

Does it feel unwanted? Correct? Necessary? Frightening? Irritating when challenged? Morally important? Doubtful?

Stance includes but is broader than the ego-dystonic/ego-syntonic distinction.

Treatment Fit

The connection between a clinical formulation and the mechanism a treatment is intended to change.

A good Treatment Fit question sounds like this:

"What is maintaining this behavior, and which part of treatment is designed to change that process?"

Trigger

The event, thought, image, sensation, uncertainty, rule violation, change, or other occurrence that starts a particular sequence.

A trigger can be internal or external.

The trigger is the first lens because the same behavior can begin from very different places.

Appendix N: Resource and Referral Guide

This guide does not endorse a particular clinician or commercial program. Organizations, services, and professional directories change, so verify current details before relying on them.

Start With the Type of Expertise

For a question involving possible OCD, look for a clinician who has specific experience assessing and treating OCD, including ERP.

For a question involving possible OCPD, look for a clinician comfortable assessing personality disorders and distinguishing traits from a full disorder.

For a question involving both, ask directly whether the clinician has experience with the OCD/OCPD differential or with complex comorbidity.

A general statement such as "I treat anxiety" does not necessarily mean the person has advanced OCD expertise.

Questions to Ask a Prospective Clinician

You can ask a clinic or therapist:

Do you assess both OCD and obsessive-compulsive personality disorder?

What experience do you have with differential diagnosis when perfectionism, checking, rigidity, and intrusive thoughts overlap?

If OCD is diagnosed, do you provide ERP or work closely with someone who does?

How do you assess personality patterns when OCD is already present?

Do you use structured interviews or standardized measures when appropriate?

How do you decide when a second diagnosis or another differential should be considered?

You do not need a clinician to use the exact vocabulary in this book.

You need someone who can explain their assessment process.

Established Information Sources

National mental health agencies, major professional organizations, recognized medical references, and peer-reviewed journals can provide reliable general information.

For OCD, national health agencies and professional psychiatric or psychological organizations commonly describe the disorder and evidence-based treatment.

For OCPD, peer-reviewed review articles and established clinical references are particularly useful because the treatment literature is smaller.

When reading online, distinguish among:

a clinical guideline,

a peer-reviewed review,

a professional information page,

a personal essay,

and a social-media post.

They can all be meaningful, but they do not carry the same evidentiary weight.

Bring Sources Without Building a Case File

If a source helped you identify a question, bring the citation or one short note.

You do not need to print every article.

A clinician is more likely to engage with:

I read that OCD and OCPD can co-occur, and I want to understand whether you see two processes in my history.

than with a folder designed to force a conclusion.

Use research to improve the question.

When Cost or Access Is a Barrier

Access to specialty mental health care varies by location, insurance, income, and health system.

Possible starting points can include primary care, community mental health services, university clinics, hospital outpatient programs, telehealth services where legally available, and professional directories.

If you cannot find a clinician with both areas of expertise, an OCD specialist may still help clarify whether a true obsession-compulsion loop is present, while a clinician experienced in personality assessment may help evaluate broader patterns.

The important point is to tell each professional what remains unanswered.

If You Are in Immediate Danger

This book is not an emergency resource.

If you are at immediate risk of harming yourself or someone else, unable to care for yourself safely, experiencing severe confusion or a sudden major change in mental state, or facing another urgent crisis, seek emergency help appropriate to your location.

A diagnostic comparison can wait.

Safety cannot.

Appendix O: The No-Score Decision Path

This page is a thinking aid, not a diagnostic flowchart.

Use it when a behavior looks "obsessive" and you are tempted to assign it immediately to OCD or OCPD.

Step 1: Describe the Behavior Without an Adjective

Write what a camera would see or what a recorder would hear.

Not: "I am obsessive about email."

Write: "After sending an email, I reopen it several times and reread the same sentence."

Not: "I am controlling with money."

Write: "I review my partner's purchases and require spending to follow the categories I created."

If you cannot describe the behavior concretely, stay at Step 1.

Step 2: Ask What Happened First

Was there an intrusive thought, image, urge, sensation, doubt, or sense of wrongness?

Was there a change, a different method, an imperfection, an unfinished task, or a rule violation?

Was there a real external risk?

Was there another trigger entirely?

Write the answer without interpreting it.

Step 3: Ask What Would Happen If You Did Nothing

This question often reveals the problem the behavior is trying to solve.

Possible answers:

"I would be afraid someone could be harmed."

"I would feel contaminated."

"I would feel that the action was incomplete."

"I would believe the work was being done improperly."

"I would be angry that the rule was ignored."

"I would worry that I looked incompetent."

"I do not know."

Each answer needs context. None is a diagnosis.

Step 4: Ask What the Behavior Changes

Does it reduce anxiety for a short time?

Does it provide reassurance that fades?

Does it restore a sense of completeness?

Does it restore a preferred standard?

Does it put you back in control of the method?

Does it solve a real practical problem?

If the immediate effect is unclear, observe one future episode rather than inventing an answer.

Step 5: Ask How Broad the Pattern Is

Is the behavior tied mainly to a small set of intrusive themes?

Does the same standard or control style appear across work, home, money, relationships, travel, and leisure?

Did it begin recently?

Has it been recognizable across much of adult life?

Reach changes the interpretation.

Step 6: Ask What the Pattern Costs

Time.

Missed deadlines.

Avoidance.

Relationship conflict.

Workplace conflict.

Exhaustion.

Reduced independence for other people.

Lost leisure.

Distress.

If the pattern creates little distress or impairment and remains flexible, a clinician may see traits or habits rather than a disorder.

Step 7: Keep Four Answers Open

After using the map, do not write only "OCD" or "OCPD."

Keep four broad possibilities:

Possible OCD process.

Possible OCPD pattern.

Possible both.

Possible neither or another explanation.

This four-answer habit is one of the simplest protections against self-diagnosis.

Step 8: Connect the Question to Treatment

If you are in treatment, ask what mechanism the current intervention targets.

If the behavior has an obsession-compulsion loop, how is the treatment changing that loop?

If the behavior is a broad standard or control pattern, how is the treatment addressing flexibility, perfectionism, interpersonal impact, or the formulation your clinician is using?

If no one can explain the connection, that is a reason to ask for review.

Step 9: Stop

The final step matters.

Do not repeat the decision path until you get the answer that feels certain.

Do not run every behavior through it.

Use it once for a representative example, record what remains unclear, and take that uncertainty to the person qualified to assess it.

The tool succeeds when it makes the clinical question smaller and more precise.

It fails when it becomes another certainty ritual.

About the Author

Evie Dove Huynh writes plain-language guides for people caught between two possible explanations for what they're experiencing.

Her books grew out of a simple observation: most self-help assumes you already know what you're dealing with. The shelves are full of books about OCD, about autism, about burnout, and almost nothing for the person still trying to work out which one applies to them. That gap is where people lose years.

She writes for the reader in that gap. Every book draws on current peer-reviewed research, cites its sources so you can check them, and explains the distinctions in language you could repeat to a doctor. She doesn't diagnose, and she's clear about that throughout. What she offers is the vocabulary and the questions to take to someone who can.

Evie writes full-time and reads more clinical literature than is strictly healthy.

About the Decoding the Overlap Series

Two conditions. One set of symptoms. Completely different answers.

Some of the most consequential questions in mental health and neurodivergence come down to telling apart two things that look almost identical from the inside. Is this OCD or is it autism? A meltdown or a panic attack? Burnout, or depression? ADHD, or something closer to bipolar?

The distinctions matter because different problems can call for different treatment targets. An intervention that is well supported for one condition may be irrelevant, incomplete, or require adaptation when a different mechanism is operating. Getting the formulation wrong can delay useful care.

Yet almost every book on the shelf begins after the question is settled. This series begins before it.

Each volume takes one pair of commonly confused conditions and lays them side by side: what each actually is, how they differ in ways you can observe in yourself, how treatment targets can change when the mechanism changes, and what to say to a clinician to get the question properly examined.

These books do not diagnose. No book can. What they offer is a clearer picture of what you might be looking at, and the language to take it to someone who can help.

The Decoding the Overlap Series: for the questions that come before the diagnosis.

References

American Psychiatric Association. (2022). *Diagnostic and statistical manual of mental disorders* (5th ed., text rev.). American Psychiatric Association Publishing. https://doi.org/10.1176/appi.books.9780890425787

American Psychiatric Association. (n.d.). *What are obsessive-compulsive and related disorders?* Retrieved August 15, 2026, from https://www.psychiatry.org/patients-families/obsessive-compulsive-disorder/what-is-obsessive-compulsive-disorder

Gecaite-Stonciene, J., Williams, T., Lochner, C., Hoffman, J., & Stein, D. J. (2022). Efficacy and tolerability of pharmacotherapy for obsessive-compulsive personality disorder: A systematic review of randomized controlled trials. *Expert Opinion on Pharmacotherapy, 23*(11), 1351-1358. https://doi.org/10.1080/14656566.2022.2100695

National Institute for Health and Care Excellence. (2005). *Obsessive-compulsive disorder and body dysmorphic disorder: Treatment* (Clinical guideline CG31). https://www.nice.org.uk/guidance/cg31

National Institute of Mental Health. (2023). *Obsessive-compulsive disorder: When unwanted thoughts or repetitive behaviors take over* (NIH Publication No. 23-MH-4676). U.S. Department of Health and Human Services, National Institutes of Health. https://www.nimh.nih.gov/health/publications/obsessive-compulsive-disorder-when-unwanted-thoughts-or-repetitive-behaviors-take-over

Pinto, A., Teller, J., & Wheaton, M. G. (2022). Obsessive-compulsive personality disorder: A review of symptomatology, impact on functioning, and treatment. *Focus, 20*(4), 389-396. https://doi.org/10.1176/appi.focus.20220058

Wheaton, M. G., Ward, H. E., & Pinto, A. (2022). Obsessive-compulsive disorder with co-occurring obsessive-compulsive personality disorder: A practice focused review. *Journal of Cognitive Psychotherapy, 36*(4), 315-326. https://doi.org/10.1891/JCP-2022-0023

Zimmerman, M. (2026). *Obsessive-compulsive personality disorder (OCPD).* MSD Manual Professional Edition.

https://www.msdmanuals.com/professional/psychiatric-disorders/personality-disorders/obsessive-compulsive-personality-disorder-ocpd

www.ingramcontent.com/pod-product-compliance
Lightning Source LLC
LaVergne TN
LVHW060546061126
851857LV00017B/1920